M000286294

6/8/21

To Brett and Kate McKay,

Thank you for having had
a positive ~~effect~~ on ~~my~~
personal and professional life

Sincerely,

Paul

Letters to Our Younger Selves

A Combat Manual

For Mindful Living

1ˢᵗ Edition

Paul F. Martino, M.S., Ph.D.

Justin R. Miller, Ph.D.

Nathan Gerowitz, D.C.

Letters to Our Younger Selves

A Combat Manual
For Mindful Living

1st Edition

Paul F. Martino, M.S., Ph.D.

Justin R. Miller, Ph.D.

Nathan Gerowitz, D.C.

Copyright © 2021 by Paul F. Martino, M.S., Ph.D., Justin R. Miller, Ph.D., Nathan Gerowitz, D.C.

All rights reserved. No part of this publication may be reproduced, distributed, or transmitted in any form or by any means, including photocopying, recording, or other electronic or mechanical methods, without the prior written permission of the publisher, except in the case of brief quotations embodied in critical reviews and certain other noncommercial uses permitted by copyright law. For permission requests, write to the author, addressed "Attention: Permissions " at DoktesInc@Gmail.com

BookBaby
www.BookBaby.com

Ordering Information:
For details, contact DoktesInc@Gmail.com

Print ISBN: 978-1-09836-7-053
eBook ISBN: 978-1-09836-7-060

Printed in the United States of America on SFI Certified paper.
First Edition

Disclaimer: This book and all of its stories and content are meant for entertainment purposes only. Details in some anecdotes and stories have been changed to protect the identity of the persons involved. If you need legal advice, financial advice, or medical and health advice we strongly recommend you contact a certified professional in that field to help you.

This book is dedicated to our late friend

Patrick Kurt Pfaffle, Ph.D.,

our teacher, leader, and friend

who taught us to serve.

CONTENTS

How To
Use This Book

Dear Reader,

Thank you for taking a leap of faith and choosing to use your valuable time to read this book. We are Paul, Justin, and Nate, and we are all highly flawed individuals. By that, we mean that we have done some pretty stupid shit over the years. Despite this, we have experienced some modest success and have been able to learn lessons we wish we would have learned earlier in life. While we do not regret any of our life choices, we often consider how growing up would have been different if we had the knowledge and experience that we have now.

We desire to share with you some of the lessons we have learned so that maybe you won't have to make the same mistakes we made. After years of giving some of this same advice to our students and patients, two things dawned on us: 1.) We can help more people than just our students and patients, and 2.) Our faces alone are not enough to make this world a better place so we should probably write a book. **We have written this book in the format of a series of letters providing advice to our younger selves, which we hope makes the advice fun and easy to read**. Each author's section stands alone, so you may read the sections in any order you wish. You will find that each of us has a very different voice.

We are all speaking from the heart, and speaking from our experience and education. The three of us independently began our lives as unremarkable people and want to provide advice that any person can use to achieve success. We have tried to include as many "gold nuggets of wisdom" as we could, as well as a few shameless recountings of our most excellent failures. If we were able to achieve success using these gold nuggets of wisdom, then so can you.

Just as a heads up, the three of us almost never take ourselves seriously, but we always take our obligations very seriously. You'll find a generous blend of irony, sarcasm, and sincerity, but if you become offended at any point please know that it wasn't intentional. Try to continue reading through the parts that you do not agree with now because considering different ideas, while sometimes irritating, may allow you to grow. **The objective of the book is to help you grow through struggling as we have.** Now, before you progress any further, here is a list of important points to remember as you read:

We have tried to focus on ordinary and common experiences. One of our favorite quotes comes from the great Pittsburgh Steelers' coach Chuck Noll. In the 1970's he coached the Pittsburgh Steelers to four Super Bowl Championships. He said, "Champions are champions not because they do anything extraordinary but because they do the ordinary things better than anyone else." We agree strongly with this sentiment.

Each letter dishes out some helpful advice. These letters are not meant to be a deep dive into the topics that the advice covers because we have found that it's too easy to get lost in long-winded explanations. All we are going to do in each letter is briefly introduce you to some of the lessons we have learned. After reading each letter, if you want to further your knowledge on these lessons, the reference section of the book is where some additional reading is suggested. This additional reading is written by people who are far smarter than we are.

Finally, we want you to be able to apply the information we share with you. We hope that the advice from our letters might help you achieve a meaningful and productive life. After reading this book, we want you to have the ability to achieve any goal, even if that goal takes you down the road less traveled. It's our pleasure to be able to share these thoughts with all of you.

Much love,

Paul, Justin, & Nate

JUSTIN'S LETTERS

1.

Struggling

Dear Justin,

For just a second, I want you to think about the people who have caused you to struggle the most in your life. Who comes to mind? What do you think of them now? Hopefully you have realized that the people who made you struggle are also the people who have caused the most personal growth in your life. Some of them caused you to struggle because they cared and wanted you to become a better, stronger person. Some of them were just obstinate bastards who wanted nothing more than to get in your way, but you know what? It doesn't matter. If you are struggling, you are also getting stronger no matter the reason.

There are a million and one clichés about struggling and personal growth i.e. "no pain no gain", "pain is temporary"; I'm sure you've heard them all. Nevertheless, despite the corny lines painted on gym walls and motivational posters everywhere, people today suck at struggling and don't understand its importance. Just recently, I was teaching a difficult concept to a small group of students, when all of the sudden one of them said to me "Why do you hate us?" Over time, these students had become so damn soft that they actually equated someone wanting to challenge them in a classroom, the safest possible environment to be challenged in, with hating them. It makes me inexplicably sad, which is why I want to make sure that you understand what to do in a struggle so you can become stronger yourself, and teach others about it too. The cycle of weakness must be stopped, and you need to do your part.

In a future letter about success, I will explain how struggling is an important process on your journey to success, and I will give you a few tools to make sure you are always moving forward after each success. In short: you need to start out humbly (or in the mud as I say), make some tangible/measurable progress, and once you have had some success get back to struggling (in a different pile of mud) so you can continue to get stronger. Before you can apply these tools, however, you first need to understand how to struggle because you can make things unnecessarily difficult for yourself if you don't take the right approach. Here is how I keep from being stuck in a struggle:

1. Be grateful for each struggle

2. Do not struggle alone

3. Know when it's time to get out of the struggle

Before moving on, I want to clarify that getting stuck during a struggle is nothing more than a mindset you should avoid simply because it doesn't get you anywhere. When you are struggling, you should instead have the mindset of climbing. Throughout this book, you will get to hear some stories about the struggles you will climb out of, such as rotisserie chicken hell and the cleaning of shitty rat cages. For today though, I would like to give you some pointers on how you can stay in that climbing mindset while working through a struggle.

First off, we've got to talk about gratitude. This topic is going to come up several times in this book, both in my letters and the letters from Paul and Nate, but it's so damn important that we are going to start talking about it right now. When you are going through a struggle, you must be grateful for it, for several reasons. First, if you are feeling too comfortable wherever you are in life, you aren't growing. That's a problem because feeling comfortable breeds complacency, and complacency breeds weakness on many levels (note: complacency is different from contentment, see Chapter 22- Chase Contentment, Not Happiness). Whether on a physiological level, psychological level, or a spiritual level, when there is no stimulus for growth, you get weaker because that is the energetically efficient thing for your body to do. It is costly to maintain strength, but it is a worthwhile investment (see Chapter 26- How to Get Strong).

Now here is another reason to be grateful for your struggles: they will grant you understanding and compassion towards others who struggle. You may not understand specifically what people must do to get through their struggle, but at the very least, you will understand what they are experiencing and be able to provide better support for them. It's always easy for me to tell when someone hasn't struggled much before, because when they do encounter a challenge, they become angry, self-centered, and act as if they are the only one who has ever experienced any difficulty, shouting things like "This isn't fair!" We all started there at some point in our lives, but the fastest way to grow out of that kind of attitude is to struggle often and be grateful for the growth.

The next part of getting through a struggle has to do with reaching out for help when you need it. This is hard for some people to do, and I can appreciate wanting to do something without help, but here is the thing: there is no bonus prize for getting through a struggle without asking for help or advice, and there is no one on this planet who has not benefited from the wisdom of outside mentors at some point in their life. I'm not saying that you should just drop everything and run to your supervisor or mentor every time you hit a snag, but I am saying that you don't have a monopoly on good ideas. Even Arnold Schwarzenegger (the great bodybuilder, actor, and former governor of California) in the Foreword section of <u>Tools of Titans</u> mentions that not even he is a self-made man. To claim so would discount the many mentors that he has had over the years including coaches, teachers, and his parents who helped him climb his way to success. Therefore, the next time you are struggling and are tempted to say "I am an adult, and adults don't ask for help, especially not from their parents," remember this: You do need help. Everyone does. Plus, parents like to hear from their spawn occasionally.

My last point about struggling is knowing when to get out. This is important because struggling when there is nothing left to gain "is just being stuck." It may be time to go a different direction, but it is often a difficult decision, because if you change directions too easily and too often, you will never accomplish anything. It will be up to you to assess whether or not to stay a course, but I use a few guidelines to make that decision easier. First, you don't make your decision to get out of a struggle when you are in a valley. Remember how we said that you need to climb through a struggle? That means there are going to be valleys, peaks, and the climbing time in-between. When you are down in the valley, it always seems like a good time to get out, because you are tired and your emotions are running wild. It's much safer to make a big decision about leaving a struggle when you are climbing up or, even better, at a peak. From way up there, you will have a much clearer picture of your situation and will be able to ask yourself the hard questions like "Is there more for me to gain in my current position?" and "Will it be worth the effort to push just a little further down this path?" If you can answer yes to both of these questions while at a high point, I think you can feel pretty confident that you are still on the right path. Answering no to either question just means you need to start weighing your options, and if ultimately you decide it's time to leave your current struggle, you can have the confidence of knowing that you did so at a high point and got the most you possibly could have out of it.

To wrap things up today, I think I will just leave you with this quote from Bruce Lee. Bruce Lee was an actor, martial artist, and philosopher during the 1960's and early 1970's. He said, "Do not pray for an easy life, pray for the strength to endure a difficult one." I like to think he was talking about the importance of being able to struggle well, and hopefully now you have a better idea of how to do that. It has certainly gotten me far over the years.

Justin

2.
Failure

Dear Justin,

Today I would like to take a few moments to follow up on my previous letter discussing how to struggle. Therein, we broke down some important ideas, not least of which is that the discomfort of struggling is a sure sign that you are getting stronger. What we did not discuss is that in some cases, the struggle may lead to something that forces growth and change in a way that nothing else can. This happens to be something that I am a foremost expert in- failure.

Now here I'm going to have to toot my own horn for a second, because when it comes to failure I'm not just pretty good at it, I am the grand-freakin-master. If failure was a form of martial arts, I would be the old guy that lives at the top of the almost impossible to climb mountain that young students journey to for training. Simply put, when it comes to failing I am one of the best.

So maybe this makes you think, "Justin, you're full of shit. If you're so good at failing, how have you made it this far through life?" Allow me to clarify- when I say that I'm great at failing, I am not just referring to the frequency of my failures, although if I tried to explain all of them, the size of this book would probably rival War and Peace. What I am actually referring to is that when I fail, I do so correctly. Today, I will introduce what I do:

1. Completely own my failure

2. Get up

3. Forgive myself for it

4. Distill the failure

It took many failures to develop these tools, and was very hard to decide which of my failures to talk about. I think one of the most important ones came when I started working for a man named Fred. Fred and his team worked in a very competitive high-stress environment. He was an extraordinary problem solver, but the problem was that he was extraordinarily awful at dealing with people. He was part of a very different generation of thinkers. It often seemed like he operated by his own set of rules and definitely had that old school mentality of just getting the job done at any personal cost. Plus, he had been around for so long; people would see his shenanigans and say things like "Oh, that's just Fred for you." That's called clout.

The first few years of working for Fred went really well; the projects were challenging but I did fine. Eventually, it was time to take the reins of my own project as all trainees do, but this is where I and many other past employees started to slip. In that fast-paced environment, in order to succeed I should have become completely immersed in the project. I needed to know absolutely everything about the project at all times. Basically, the project needed to become my life, but I really missed the boat on that one. Instead, I would just show up, help with the mandatory parts and then just leave. Maybe I would glance at the results of the day's work, or maybe I wouldn't. I would get home every day at about 3 or 4 and then just do whatever the hell I felt like. Life was just grand.

This went on for a while, I don't remember how long exactly, but eventually Fred started to take notice of my half-assery and got pissed. Really pissed. Instead of just telling me that I was not living up to his expectations, he started to completely ignore my existence. Our team would be having a meeting to review the tasks, and instead of just addressing me directly, Fred would turn to the person sitting next to me and say things like "Justin needs to do this project today," which is how he would ignore people with whom he was upset. Eventually I realized something was very wrong. For weeks, I tried desperately to get his attention or approval, but he would continually ignore me unless it was to say something derogatory. It was completely dehumanizing.

The stress of this all really started to get to me, until finally I made a mistake that caused our team to lose weeks of progress. Fred finally decided to use this moment as a learning experience for me, and that's when the ass-kicking began. Fred had a real talent for this. Never before had I been so verbally degraded. With words alone, he turned my ass inside out, upside down, shaved it with a cheese grater, and booted it into the next dimension. In addition, Fred wasn't the only one; this came from everyone involved with the project. You must remember that this was still a time where people in general were tougher and had thicker skin, and fragility was simply not an option (see Chapter 20- Don't Be Thin Skinned).

So just like that, I went from happily cruising along to being a complete dumpster fire of a person. I was a wreck. I was face-down in my apartment, both figuratively and literally, and was clearly at a crossroad. I had invested nearly three years into this training, so quitting wasn't a great option, although it was tempting after feeling as if I just got ground into subatomic particles. Slowly, I started to pick up the pieces and, for once, took the time to think about each of them. This is what led me to start developing the tools for failing well, although I did not know that's what I was doing at the time.

I first realized that when I have failed, the first/most important thing to do is take complete ownership of it. This is important because under no circumstance will blaming someone else for a fail allow you to grow and learn. Sure, I could have sat back and said none of this would have happened if Fred hadn't acted like an unreasonable a-hole and just explained to me what I was doing wrong. However, that was irrelevant. The point was that I screwed up, and accepting responsibility for <u>my</u> part in any failure was the stimulus for growth. There will certainly be circumstances where other people will have played some role in your failures, but that is not what matters. When you fail, treat that failure like it's your baby. It might be an ugly one, but you are responsible for it.

Then the next step is to get up. It sounds cliché, but you have to do it. Notice that I put owning failure before getting up. Accepting responsibility for your actions is essential for entering that growth mindset that provides the stable footing you need for standing up after taking a big hit. So when I say get up, I do mean physically- you will eventually have to turn off that streaming service you have been binge watching. Nevertheless, getting up also means you are preparing yourself to learn and <u>let go of that fear of failing again</u>.

Now most everyone has a fear of failure at some level. Have you ever wondered why people, including myself, just love watching fail videos? I mean, some of them are just plain old funny, but I also think it's why people like watching horror movies. Watching other people experience things that we find scary is exhilarating! But I digress. It's very important that you push past the fear of that particular failure: Accept that it may happen again, and do not let the fear of failure hold you back. If you can't accept it, you are not ready to get up yet.

I still struggle mightily with this next step in recovering from failure. Part of processing a failure is eventually <u>forgiving yourself</u>. Have you ever screwed something up, big or small, and then spent days replaying it over and over in your head? Alternatively, maybe something you said publicly just came out wrong, and you spent way too much time thinking, "What kind of dumbass would say that?" Well, I think it's natural to recoil back at ourselves for failure, but insisting on punishing ourselves over and over for the same past failure is completely unproductive. It's like paying interest on a loan that you do not owe. Instead channel all that otherwise wasted energy into the last step: distilling the failure.

In case you don't know, distillation is simply a process of extraction. When you have a mixture of substances, you can use distillation to separate out some while leaving others behind. This works for failure because it's definitely a mixture of a whole lot of suck with a bit of valuable experience in there. If you don't apply this method, two things will likely happen: 1.) You will take way too much suck with you; 2.) You will probably miss what you were supposed to learn and make the same mistake again. So for me, if I hadn't taken the time to separate out the parts of my failure, this is probably what I would have concluded from it: 1.) Freds a dick; 2.) That's pretty much it.

So what is the key to a good extraction? Well this is going to be anti-climactic because it's completely simple. First, you find the root cause of the failure. In my case, I was able to find the root cause after a lot of personal reflection. Just by finally stopping and thinking about my situation for once, I realized that I needed to just drop the ego and admit that I really had no idea how to work independently. That should have been obvious, but I was so distracted by all that bitterness toward everyone involved in the situation that I nearly missed it. That's why it's so important to distill the failure. Also, there is no shame in getting input from someone with some expertise, or at least someone with an outside perspective to help you find the root cause of your failure. Chances are, as you were on the way to failing these people were already trying to advise you, but you weren't listening. I know I wasn't.

Next, you need to change your course of action. Nothing is more frustrating than when I see a student hit a wall when faced with a challenge, and then get up (which is good) but then run head first into the same exact spot on that wall, and then again, and again. If you don't, actually act on preventing what caused that failure in the first place it will happen repeatedly. It sounds totally simple, and it is, but you would not believe how often people forget to do something differently. Some people today seem to have a lot of difficulty pivoting, but that is a topic for another time.

So there you have it- the art of failing, or a summary of it. I understand that each of these tools is very difficult to use and develop. They all require you to look at failure straight in the face, and that is no small task. I also don't expect that just a few paragraphs on each of these steps will be sufficient for you to know exactly what to do with each failure, which is why I will continue to write and give you more tools for dealing with failure.

Justin

3.
Self-Discipline

Dear Justin,

Do you have self-discipline yet? Well if not, you will soon have some painful experiences that will teach you a lot about this subject. One of these experiences will have you ready to choke someone over some hard-boiled eggs, but before we get to that, do you really know what it means to be self-disciplined?

At the outset, being self-disciplined has similarities to being committed, and commitment forms the basis of some important things in life (i.e. having a good marriage and career). Commitment is not just a feeling, but is the conscious decision to overcome all obstacles. This decision does not waver no matter what your feelings are, whom you are dealing with, or what the weather is like. Understanding what it means to be committed is an important aspect of being disciplined; however, self-discipline has a few more layers that I would like to unpack.

First off, the commitment side of discipline is actually the simplest part to understand- it gives us the fortitude to make a major and long-term change in some aspect of our behavior. This is valuable in its own right, but the added benefit of becoming self-disciplined is that it allows us to make these changes in a way that is more balanced and flexible. Don't get me wrong, there are certain things in which you should be exclusively committed, but there are some habits such as studying, working, resting, and exercising which self-discipline allows for a healthier lifestyle. I will explain why in a moment, but first, here are the tools I use for developing self-discipline:

1. Get "chained" to what is important to you

2. Have planned and controlled relapses

3. Install an off-switch

So, getting chained- what does that mean? I can't take credit for this one, but this is the part of self-discipline that is most similar to commitment. The concept comes from Pastor Steven Furtick from Elevation Church. He is a man who is not afraid to discuss the fact that while he is a pastor he is still very much just a man. He still gets pissed off about things and occasionally thinks about throttling his enemies, but he has learned how to prevent such feelings from getting the best of him.

In his sermon "Choosing Your Chains" he outlines how it is possible to get "chained" to damaging habits such as being offended (See Chapter 20- Don't Be Thin Skinned) or feeling bitterness, but then points out it works exactly the same way for making positive changes like having faith and treating others with grace and respect. In both cases, it all begins with a **Choice**. It might seem like a tiny insignificant choice at the time, but that is where being chained begins and <u>so does developing self-discipline</u>.

For most, making the initial choice to make a positive change in your life isn't really the hardest part of developing self-discipline. It's easy to get up and say, "Today I will go to the gym" or "Today I will not be a douche to that barista who is unnaturally happy for 7AM." The hard part is actually putting your choice into practice (See Chapter 11: Gratitude), but there is a silver lining. Once you have practiced your choice a few times, it eventually becomes a <u>H</u>abit; it becomes a behavior that takes little thought until you don't even have to make a choice anymore. At that point, your new behavior has become <u>A</u>utomatic. It's the new baseline setting, and before long, it becomes more than just something that you do. It becomes part of who you are, or part of your <u>I</u>dentity. When something has been a part of your identity for long enough, it simply becomes your <u>N</u>ature, as if that behavior was encoded in your DNA. Now we can put it all together:

<u>C</u>hoice

<u>H</u>abit

<u>A</u>utomatic

<u>I</u>dentity

<u>N</u>ature

It all started out with just one little decision to make a small change in your behavior, which led to you becoming CHAINed to that same behavior which you no longer need to think about. You just do it. I strongly recommend listening to the sermon, but first we have more work to do: we need to talk about where commitment and self-discipline diverge.

Commitment is black and white, you are or you aren't committed. For behaviors in which you develop self-discipline, your level of dedication can exist on a spectrum: there will be times when you are very strict and others when you have a controlled relapse. You may even choose to take a break from that behavior entirely, both of which are completely healthy. It is up to you to determine which habits to commit to and which to develop self-discipline for, but there are some that clearly belong in one category versus the other. For example, you do not take a break from being committed to your spouse, unless you are an asshole, but you aren't. On the other hand, you should take a break from exercising to give your body time to rest and recover, and if you do, you will get more out of it. Here is an example of what can happen if you don't practice the rest and relapse part of self-discipline.

During your undergraduate years, you will become involved with amateur bodybuilding competitions. Before I explain what happened, let me just make two things very clear. First, just being able to compete as a bodybuilder is a great accomplishment. It requires a great deal of sacrifice through your diet and exercise regimes, but that's just the nature of bodybuilding. Second, I do recognize that bodybuilding is an extreme example, and not many go down that path. It does, however, provide an example of how you risk doing damage to your personal or professional relationships, or at the least, start acting completely irrational when you commit to something that is healthier to be self-disciplined.

One moment will really stand out to you as you are working through the final weeks of cutting down for your first competition. The blandness of the diet alone is enough to make some people quit since at this point, it involves mainly very low carbohydrate foods and lean proteins such as egg whites from hard boiled eggs. Basically only things with no flavor whatsoever are on the list. There will be about three weeks left, at which you will have gotten down to about 8% body fat. That's pretty lean, but for a bodybuilder it's rather unremarkable which is why the pressure will really start to rise. One day, you will be walking back from a class which was all about chlorophyll (I think, you will spend most of the lecture thinking about when you can have your next hardboiled egg.), and you will stop in the dormitory cafeteria to pick up said eggs. Let me just explain for a second how sick you will be of eggs. You will hate them so much that you will become convinced that all hardboiled eggs at some point emerged from the putrid soils of hell, and that every time you eat one another demon gets its wings. However, at the same time, these eggs will be the only thing sustaining you, and keeping you from complete starvation induced madness.

After you walk into the cafeteria, you get into the buffet line only to find that the container, which usually has the eggs, is empty. You will look behind the counter to see that these eggs are there, but still cooling in a vat of water.

Clearly they had just recently been belched from the bowels of hell, OK, no problem. You will kindly ask the young woman working the line if you could just have a couple. Her response: "No, you don't need no eggs." You will try again by explaining that you just want two eggs and that's all. Again: "Nope."

Now, this is where a person who is balanced and in control would think maybe there is a good reason why this woman is being such an egg tyrant. Maybe the eggs are still hot, and they have a policy against putting out food above serving temperature. It is also possible that this woman is also feeling a bit drained and just didn't feel like complying. Nevertheless, at this point, you will be way past thinking normally. You will consider several options including throwing a chair through the glass so you can get to the eggs, or making some kind of threat, but instead you will opt to make a scene: "JUST GIVE ME THE DAMN EGGS." Now everyone is looking. The managers have come out, and someone is probably calling the campus police about some psycho who looks like a shriveled up piece of beef jerky in the "caf" demanding eggs. She will eventually give you them, but not until after calling you a few much deserved choice words.

Does that sound like someone who is in control to you? Alternatively, maybe you are thinking, didn't you say before that bodybuilding is an extreme example? Of course, the dieting would cause someone to act like an idiot! However, have you ever seen an adult throw a temper tantrum over something small, like an incorrect coffee order or running out of soymilk for their latte? I bet you have at least a few times. Some of those people may just be unreasonable by nature; however, I prefer to give most humans the benefit of the doubt and believe that many of them are just overly stressed because they haven't self-disciplined their work habits. They have simply forgotten to have a rest and relapse from their responsibilities, which is what makes it possible to maintain a high level of performance for an extended period.

Bodybuilders did figure this out. It has long been known that maintaining a strict diet and training plan is not only bad for your sanity, but also decreases your metabolism making it harder and harder to get lean. This is why the "cheat day" was invented. There are many ways to do this, but in general, for one day every so often you get to have roughly twice as many carbohydrates as you would normally have, and you may even include something sugary, like half a grapefruit. Once the day is done, you then return to your normal dieting routine. So essentially, the cheat day is a controlled relapse. You still monitor how much you deviated from the diet, and you always return to your normal routine. Your "chain" will be there to pull you back in (in a good way).

Unfortunately, you won't learn about the cheat day until your second or third competition, but let me tell you, just by sliding back to a less strict level of self-discipline for one day, you will be able to think clearly again, and the next few workouts will be the best that you will have in a while. Your grades won't suck nearly as much as without cheat days, and you can make it through your cut down phases without frightening children and animals. What's my point here? The point is that allowing yourself to dial back your discipline for just a short planned period will allow you to maintain on average a very high level of performance while remaining in complete control. This works, no matter what you are doing.

For my last point on self-discipline, making sure to install an off switch is important. This is just my way of telling you that if you want to be a high performer, you will need to take a complete break from your self-disciplined behavior every so often. There are some genetic freaks out there who do not appear to need breaks and can work 80-120 hours a week without rest, but the average person does need breaks (see Chapter 23: Work Hard). The benefits are the same as the controlled relapse, but greater. It will be up to you to decide when the appropriate time is, what kind of interval to use, and how to get that rest. I can assure you that it will be worthwhile.

Now to wrap things up here, I want you to know that you will go on to win that first bodybuilding competition so the sacrifice will be worth it, but there will be a few pieces to pick up afterwards. Using these tools to develop self-discipline in the areas of your life that you find important will help you to achieve great things while maintaining better physical health, mental clarity, and personal relationships. Just practice the habit you want to be self-disciplined in until it's just part of you, dial it back a little every so often, and don't forget to rest (See Chapter 14: Rest).

Justin

4.
Meekness: Quiet Strength

Dear Justin,

Wouldn't it have been nice if as soon as you turned 18, you received a book called "How To Be An Adult" which contained the solutions to all your problems, like what you should be when you grow up, and how to act normal? Well if such a book exists, your copy must be stuck in customs somewhere because I am still waiting for it. That's ok though, because I'm going to let you in on a little secret: most everyone starts out knowing very little and has no choice but to make it up as they go. All you can do is just get through life as best as you can and take your lumps as they come. Trust me; you are going to get a lot of them. By the time you get to where I am sitting, you will have so many lumps your head will feel like someone tried to write a book in braille on it.

What have all these lumps taught me about "how to be an adult?" Telling you to just stop acting like an idiot is a bit vague and lacks direction, so I spent some time thinking about the qualities of all the people whom I consider to be "adults," and found two that they seem to have in common. The first quality was obvious: they have strength. Not just in one aspect of their lives, but in several. The second common quality was more surprising- in addition to being strong, they are also meek. Now before you walk away, just give me a second to unpack this one. I am not contradicting myself because when I say meek I do not mean weak. They are two very different things. A person who is weak is lacking in fortitude, either physical or mental, but a person who is meek could be the strongest person in the room but has control over their strength. In others words, they have <u>bridled strength</u>. Their strength is a tool that they can choose how much to use, depending on the situation.

Think about if you were in a work-related meeting, and employees were clearly unprepared which caused your supervisor to blow their top. Would you look at that supervisor and say that person looks like a strong leader? Probably not. That person is clearly not lacking in force, but do they appear to be in control of it? Probably not. Now let's use the same example, except this time the supervisor delivers a calm yet firm reprimand with clear expectations for how to move forward. That sounds much more like a supervisor that people would respect, one who has bridled strength. They have redirected those in need without excessive force or demoralizing the entire group. I believe that this is the way that all adults should behave, and being able to do so will open many doors for you.

Having bridled strength is not just about handling authority with grace, but also involves knowing how and when to follow, and being able to transition between the two roles fluidly. A person with bridled strength is comfortable with not always being in charge, and can thrive when both giving instruction and receiving it. If you are to develop bridled strength, you need to practice:

1. Being patient with those who are counting on you

2. Being teachable by those who have knowledge that you do not

I know these things sound simple, but being able to do both takes more strength than you might expect.

Let's start with being patient with those who are counting on you. I chose the wording "those who are counting on you" because when you have a position of authority such as the employer, the adult in the room, or maybe both, those around you will be counting on you for many things such as guidance, instruction, protection, to name a few. You need to treat them with patience and respect, all while making your expectations very clear. When one of your students/children/employees has not met your expectations, start by taking ownership of whether you played any part in the mistake. You can't take the fall with them every time, but be sure to ask yourself "Did I explain clearly enough what I needed?" and also "Have my expectations changed without them knowing?" Asking these questions before you react will help put the brakes on if you become frustrated with your team. Acknowledging if you did play a role in the mistake is a great way of building mutual respect.

The next part of being patient with those who are counting on you is paying attention to what kinds of motivation they respond. Remember when we played high school lacrosse, and the coach tried to motivate everyone by telling us how much we sucked, and were weak, and all those other non-Politically Correct (PC) things that you just can't really say anymore? Yeah. That one went over like a ton of bricks, and did absolutely nothing to motivate us. It's not always easy to read people and understand what motivates them, but the important thing is that if you see your strategy is not working, please do <u>try something else</u>. Don't just keep beating your head (or theirs) against the wall. Body language is your friend when learning how someone responds to motivation, and I always try to start with the carrot (positive reinforcement). There will certainly be times when the stick (negative reinforcement) is the only option, just make sure to keep it under control.

Now I would like to move on to what it means to be teachable. This is hard for some because it requires a certain degree of submissiveness, but if you are truly strong, you will have the confidence to hand over the reins every so often. Having difficulty giving up control of a leadership position is a sure sign of weakness because it suggests that you are insecure. Being teachable also requires you to check your ego and recognize when someone knows more than you do- just remember that you do not have a monopoly on good ideas. When you need to assume the role of "student," do so wholeheartedly. Leave behind any biases you may have about who is teaching you, whether they are younger than you or are maybe less experienced. None of that matters. If that person has something for you to learn, accept their instruction, be attentive, and thank them for the education.

So now, we can circle back to having the ability to seamlessly transition between a leadership position and one of a follower. It's perfectly natural to prefer one role to the other, but the point is that when you have bridled strength, you are meek, and you understand how to succeed in either position. No matter where you are, you will be able to better the lives of those around you and all you have to do is be kind and compassionate with your students, and remember to be a good student yourself.

Justin

5.

Speaking Without Getting Punched in the Face Immediately

Dear Justin,

I am here to talk to you about good ol' fashion face-to-face talking to a real person because good communication is a keystone skill in life. I would also argue, however, that you could get pretty far by saying very little and just listening. Someone once said, "It's better to remain silent and have people suspect you are an idiot, than to open your mouth and remove all doubt." Nonetheless, we all must find our voice in life if you wish to contribute to society, so when you do decide to speak, make sure you do it with authority and conviction.

Speaking with authority isn't always just about knowing the most about a subject, although having expertise (see Chapter 24: Read Often) will certainly help you feel more confident. A big part of speaking with authority is speaking in a way that is easy for people to listen. We all speak with our own unique style and trying to change that can be pretty awkward, so here are a few simple pointers that are useful, no matter what your style is or who you are speaking to:

1. Take a breath and think before you speak

2. Explain simply

3. Speak the way you write

Like always, these are really simple tools to improve your speaking that you might take for granted, but there will come a time in your future when you accidentally tell the head of a major research department that his earlier work basically amounted to nothing in front of about 50 people. Well that's what happens when you forget to take a moment to think before you speak.

I think that part of why this has become a problem is because people are <u>deathly</u> afraid of silence in a conversation and even more so in a public speaking presentation. That's why it has been dubbed the "awkward silence" but it's still a whole lot less awkward than being called out for bullshitting. All you have to do is practice taking a moment to process what is being said to you. The pause will feel much longer than it actually is, but it gives you a moment to think either "Yes, I have the expertise to answer this question/ contribute to this conversation," or "I really don't know anything about that." In that latter case, it's perfectly acceptable to admit that you are not an expert on the subject. A simple "I don't know much about that, could you tell more about..." is a safe way of keeping the conversation going if you are put on the spot because 1.) It shows interest in the subject; 2.) It's better to be consciously uninformed than unconsciously incompetent; 3.) It's much better than getting 200 words into a bullshit explanation with no way out. Of course, this will come up much less frequently if you take the time to become well-read.

Becoming well read is a subject that Paul explains in detail, but here I would like to reiterate that it is the responsibility of all adults to be able to understand what is going on around them. Whether the current issue is personal, political, or scientific you need to be able to understand it so you can <u>explain it in the simplest terms possible</u>. This does not mean becoming an expert in everything, but when you find something that is important to you, you need to be able to explain it in a way that everyone understands. It is tempting to latch on to some really complicated sounding jargon when you are first learning about a subject, even when you don't fully understand it. Many people feel that doing this will increase their credibility and show off their vocabulary, but a smart person who is listening can usually see through the smoke and mirrors.

Instead, when you are thinking about how to explain something, the trigger question that I use now is, "If I had to explain this to a 5th grader, what would I say?" This works 95% of the time. If you are speaking to an expert, they will appreciate a simple explanation. If you are just having a casual conversation, people will want to listen because it makes them feel smart. It's why people like to listen to the renowned astrophysicist Neil deGrasse Tyson; you don't walk away feeling like you are an idiot, you think, "Wow, I actually understand something complicated."

Now, to wrap things up, I want to talk a bit about speaking mechanics. There are two bad habits that I would like to address: a constant interrogative tone and words of dysfluency. To clarify, an interrogative tone is the tone to ask a question, and words of dysfluency are "um, like, and you know." This is where "speak how you write" comes in. Just imagine if this entire book was written to include every "like" or "um" that people would typically say, and every sentence ended in a question mark. You would probably get three pages into the book before you doused it with gasoline and set it on fire. It, um, would be, like, totally annoying, you know? And not only are these speaking habits annoying, using them too much will really damage your credibility. Here's a classic example. Try reading this aloud including all the pauses and interrogative tones:

Mom: Where were you last night?

You: Um…out with my friends?

Mom: What were you doing?

You: Uh…hanging out?

Guilty until proven innocent, when all you were really doing was playing Dungeons and Dragons with your friends.

Removing all of these habits from your speech is definitely challenging, and we all use them to varying degrees. Remember that girl in your undergraduate political science class who said "You know what I'm sayin'" 27 times in one explanation. So instead of trying to quit them all cold turkey, start by becoming conscious of when you are using them. Remind yourself of the opposite of an interrogative statement, which is the declarative statement. I know declaring something to be true, is like, totally, scary, but it is an important part of speaking with authority. Also, becoming aware of when you are using words of disfluency will go a long way towards using them less and less.

Well, this is a lot to think about, and changing any part of the way you speak is very uncomfortable, so don't try to incorporate all these changes at once. Doing so would cause you to become so uptight that every time someone asks you a question, you would start making diamonds in your rectum. Instead, just focus on each tip individually: Think before speaking so you know when and when not to speak; explain simply; speak with as few filler words as humanly possible

All of these things will take work, but I promise it will be worthwhile. To quote the American poet and educator Taylor Mali, "Contrary to the wisdom of the bumper sticker, it's not enough these days to simply "question authority." You've got to speak with it too."

Justin

6.
Emailing Without Getting Punched in the Face Later

Dear Justin,

It's funny how easy it is to judge someone just because they didn't choose the right words, or they asked a question the wrong way, isn't it? Yet we all do it. So like it or not, in order to be successful in all stages of life you need to make sure you learn how to communicate effectively. This doesn't mean that you need to become some kind of master wordsmith, but you do need to understand the basics of clear, respectful communication on multiple platforms (email and in person). Since we have already discussed in-person communication in my last letter, today I would like to focus on improving just one other form of communication: email. Developing this skill will set you apart from your peers, so it is definitely a worthwhile endeavor.

Putting together emails is something we all do often, so it's easy to get sloppy. Here I am going to give you a few reminders to reduce the number emails you send to any future supervisors/employers that cause them to roll their eyes so hard they dislocate a retina. Today we will be focusing on writing an email to a supervisor when you need to ask for something. First, I will give you a few tools to help you structure this type of email, and then we will break down an actual example of how <u>not</u> to do it. Here are the tools:

1. Address the recipient appropriately

2. Clearly state the who, what, and why for the email

3. Show gratitude for their time

4. Keep communication lines open

Remember, these four tools are just the bare minimum that you should use to construct a solid email, but now let's get to our unfortunate example. I am going to show you an email from a future student of yours, a very young one, so be compassionate. I think when you communicate exclusively via electronic means it's easy to forget that there is an actual person on the other end, a potentially very tired, irritable, or irrational person. Unlike us, many people today did not grow up mainly communicating in person where you have the threat of immediately being punched by that big-boned kid who lives a few houses down, but that definitely doesn't mean that poor electronic communication has no consequences. You just might not feel the consequences immediately.

To give you some more background on this student's email, one day you will be the instructor of a class, which is challenging and requires a strong science background. There is usually a waiting list to get into the course, so students who have all the prerequisites are given preference and those who do not are let in on a case-by-case basis, only if they have taken related classes. One particular year the class filled up quickly, which was not unusual, but then this email came in:

Hi

So I'm a junior marketing major and I am very interested in joining your class. I see the class is completely full and I don't have any of the prerequisites. I'm also not the greatest at chemistry. Kate may or may not have told me that the prerequisites aren't actually necessary to take/do well in the class. So if that's the case can you add me?

Thanks!

OK, first of all: Worst. Marketing. Major. Ever. Now that I've gotten that off my chest, let's go through the good, the bad, and the ugly, starting with how this student addressed me. We live in a business casual world, so it can be a little hard to tell how formal to be when opening an email, but here are two pointers. First, always use the recipient's actual name, if nothing else to get their attention amidst the many junk emails that we all get. Second, if it's a superior that you are addressing, it's usually a good idea to include an honorific such as Mr. or Ms., Dr., or Professor. People with these sorts of titles usually had to be crapped on quite a bit to earn them. To quote our favorite movie villain, Dr. Evil, from Austin Powers: International Man of Mystery -"That's Doctor Evil. I didn't spend six years in evil medical school to be called Mr., Thank you very much."

Now let's move on to the three W's, which are <u>Who</u> you are (if you aren't already acquainted), <u>What</u> you want, and <u>Why</u> (the rationale) the person who you are emailing should give you what you want. This student does ok with the first two parts; he introduces himself (sort of) and makes it very clear that he would like to join the class. Where he really fails is in the rationale. Any time you ask for anything, no matter how small, just remember that it's still a negotiation. In the example, I appreciate the student's honesty about not being good with chemistry, but saying that he heard from so-and-so that the prerequisites aren't real, was definitely the wrong approach. One might not want to unintentionally call the professor or the department liars. Maybe we can get into negotiation tactics in another letter, but for now just remember to use a bit of common sense. I would have been perfectly satisfied if the student had written something like "I'm not too good at chemistry, but I am dedicated and will work hard to succeed." Nothing fancy, but that would have made the request seem much more reasonable.

Next up we have to discuss showing gratitude, which is not just about thanking the recipient for their time, but recognizing what you are really asking for. It could just be their time, it could be a company resource, or in this case, it was asking me to put my professional reputation on the line by bending the rules. To address this, the student could have said, "I fully recognize that you would be making an exception for me, but I would be very grateful for the opportunity to be in your class." So next time you are going to ask someone for a favor via email, before pressing send, take a few moments to think about what you are really asking that person to give you in order to fulfill your request, and for God's sake proofread the email.

Finally, let's wrap up this email by keeping our lines of communication open. This is an easy one. By simply stating something like "If needed, I would be happy to discuss this more in person," you 1.) Demonstrate that you are not a coward, and that you can ask for things while not hiding behind a computer screen; 2.) Send the message that you are confident that what you are asking for is reasonable. Just make sure you make good on it if they do want to talk. Lastly, some people prefer to close with some light small talk such as "I hope you are having a good week" or something like that, just don't overdo it. You could put this up front, but ending with it tends to sound a bit more sincere. There, that wasn't so hard! Let's try putting all these new components together to see how its sounds:

Hi Professor Justin

I am currently a junior marketing major and I am very interested in joining your class. I see that the class is full and I don't have any of the prerequisites. I'm also not the greatest at chemistry, but I am dedicated and will work hard to succeed. I fully recognize that you would be making an exception for me, but I would be very grateful for the opportunity to be in your class. If needed, I would be happy to discuss this more in person.

I hope you are having a great semester and thanks for your time!

And there you have it- it's not a perfect email, but it's short, to the point, and certainly less cringe worthy than the first version. Also notice that I put this email together without the use of any sort of emoticons. I recognize their usefulness in clarifying your tone when sending an informal email, but if the overall structure and content of your email sucks, no amount of smiley-face-unicorns can save you. So just to review, when you need to ask for something via email, remember to address the person to whom you are asking with respect, state your request and why it's reasonable. Also, be grateful for the time/resources/clout needed to fulfill the request, and offer to speak about it in person. Just remember: the main goal is to send an email that is clear and not offensive. It's possible that the reader happens to be having a bad day, or maybe they just haven't had their coffee yet. Maybe deep down they are actually criminally insane. Without being there to see them, you just can't be sure.

Justin

7.

Success at Long Last

Dear Justin,

I am very happy to tell you that later in life; you will experience success. It's modest and I don't want to give you too many spoilers, but I will say that you learn quickly that success is not an endpoint. In your life, success will be more of a noteworthy landmark that you reach now and again on a journey filled with struggling and failure as you pursue your life's goals. I have already discussed the latter two with you in earlier letters, so today we are going to complete the cycle by discussing success.

Success is a hard topic to add anything new to because there is lots of "How to Succeed" information out there and there are others who have already done an excellent job of compiling the routines and habits of some world-class performers (Reading Assignment: Tools of Titans by Tim Ferriss). All that I can offer you for now are a few tips to give you a springboard for starting your journey towards success and for continually growing into a better, more accomplished human after each success. For everything in-between, I recommend that you re-read my other letters on struggling and failure. Here are the tools to start your journey:

1. Don't be afraid to start in the mud

2. Make sure you get out of the mud

3. After you have succeeded, start struggling again (get into a different patch of mud)

Today, I find that many people have two major weaknesses: 1.) They are unwilling to start out with the humble jobs; and 2.) They mistakenly believe that their first few successes in life will be sufficient to achieve the same level of success that their parents have. Well unfortunately, after you get your diploma or that first job out of college, there will not be a guy wearing cool sunglasses who looks like/sounds like Morgan Freeman waiting to say congratulations, shake your hand, and give you the keys to a new house and luxury vehicle. When this inevitably doesn't happen, I hear all kinds of excuses for why these people haven't gotten what they expected, such as a bad economy or there are no jobs for people with my degree. What many don't realize is that each success, while it should be recognized and celebrated, is actually a checkpoint on a much longer journey that not only starts in the mud (humbly) but often leads back to a new pile of mud. It's the only way you keep growing stronger. In our case though, instead of starting in the mud, it might be more accurate to say we start in the shit.

I'm sure you will remember all of the humble jobs we had over the years, like the one at the pizza place. The Italian guy in charge had some serious anger issues, but he did make a fine pizza. Each of those jobs had something for you to learn, but they were mostly just for a little cash to goof off with friends. Really, the first job you will have that will be a significant step toward success will be when you go to work with Dad at the animal hospital. Your main responsibility will be to clean cages in the kennel, and it will be hard and dirty work, but you must be grateful for it! With the experience of starting out at the bottom, you will learn to appreciate each small success of your own, or to appreciate the struggles of others who are still at the bottom.

Working with Dad will be a great experience for other reasons too, not least of which is getting to see what a mature work ethic looks like. When it comes to work ethic/stamina, Dad is kind of a freak and I'm glad we have those genetics. In Chapter 18: Think Like an Immigrant, Paul discusses the immigrant hard work ethic and this certainly applies with Dad. He will teach you that you can't be content at the bottom and that even after you have succeeded, there will still be struggling to further your success. These lessons will be very important for the next few years of your life, which is why they are my next two topics.

After several years of spending summers cleaning kennels, you will eventually get yourself out of the mud/shit by starting your undergraduate studies. I can say with absolute certainty that being a student is a cushy job. You will work hard, but there will be a healthy dose of general dumbassery, along with very little actual responsibility. You will figure out early on what it takes to make it through while keeping things well in perspective. A test is just a test. After some hard work and some good times, you will experience your first real success when you graduate with your undergraduate degree, but here is a spoiler: Morgan Freeman will not be there, and there will be no keys to your Corvette (not that you will ever get one). The only thing to do at this point will be to get into a new pile of mud.

This pattern of success will repeat itself several times throughout your life. For example, one of the first jobs you will take out of college will be as a research technician in a lab studying diabetes. The job description will read something like "Skilled laboratory technician needed to assist with cutting edge diabetes research" which translates to "Guy needed to clean rat shit out of rat cages." OK fine, so you will be back at the bottom. You will also know by then that you can't stay there long-term, so after a while, you try to pull yourself out of mud by accepting a pharmaceutical technician job at a large grocery store. Sounds great, doesn't it? Too bad, you'll never find out, because on the first day of that job, you will learn that the pharmacy position is no longer available. Your boss tells you not to worry, they got you covered. There will be a really important job opening in the service deli.

Earlier on, I said that you need to be grateful for the humble jobs that you have, and you will be grateful for this one. Eventually. This job should probably be no more than just a footnote in your life, except for the fact this will be quite possibly the worst, most degrading job you will ever have, and definitely should appear on Mike Rowe's show, Dirty Jobs, so I'm going to tell you about it. Your main responsibility will be cooking rotisserie chickens, which you are not above doing, but the people there will find it hilarious that the guy with a four-year degree is working in the deli. In addition, that environment! The environment will have you begging for more animal cages to clean. We'll just start there.

Did you know that chicken grease could be aerosolized? Well it can, especially in that nice balmy 100°F kitchen you will be working in. It's going to get everywhere- on your face, hands, hair and all sorts of other places where chicken grease should never go. The floor will also have a healthy dose of grease, which is why each step you take will carry the risk of a fall induced skull fracture. Next, you have the industrial rotisserie oven, which will be your responsibility. It's an impressive piece of machinery and can cook chickens just fast enough to keep up with people's orders. You are going to be cranking these things out for 10 hours a day, grabbing them out the oven and pulling them off the skewers as fast as you can. The problem will be that the only oven gloves available will be made of cloth which scalding hot grease will go right through. The holes in the gloves probably won't help either, but that's only the half of the job. Since you will be working so hard to keep up with the orders, you will have to pull chickens out of their boxes still frozen and jam them down on those rusty skewers. The gloves won't help much with the cold either, so basically all day long you will go back and forth between burning and then freezing the crap out of your hands for hours. I'm sure I still have nerve damage from that. You can try to ask a manager for a new set of gloves, but he will just walk off and not come back for the rest of the day.

That brings me to the next delight of the job: the people. I'm really not sure what their major malfunction was, but just know they are going to have it out for you. At one point, one of them will try to tell you that there are so many rotisserie orders that there's no time to take a lunch break, but he has a solution. What you should do is take some chicken wings out of the fryer and set them in the garbage so you can eat. That way if management comes by, it wouldn't look like it was anyone's lunch that had been placed there. From the look on that guy's face, it will be pretty obvious that he just wants to see if you will actually eat out of the garbage. But here's the thing: you will be tired, fed up, fucking hungry, and you will already have a history of doing irrational things while hungry (See Chapter 3: Self-Discipline). That jackass will be disgusted when you hammer down those wings, but the good thing is from this point on, everyone will leave you alone. They will understand that you don't just ride the crazy train. You are the conductor.

I know this all sounds pretty terrible, and it will be for a time, but you can take solace in two things: 1.) Those people are probably still swimming in chicken grease to this day; 2.) You will be able to pull yourself out of that mess. On a particularly low day, you will get an invitation for a microbiologist position at a medical product company. It will be a great job with good pay, benefits, and a supportive supervisor. For the first time, you will be able to cruise for a bit while you build up your savings and eventually take the Graduate Record Exam (GRE). This will allow you to be accepted into a doctoral graduate program, which will most definitely be the greatest success in your life thus far. You will have access to people who are much smarter than you and are invested in your success. It will be an amazing experience, but before you get to all that pomp and circumstance, you will have to go back to being a low man on the totem pole, and this program will involve some lab animal care. What does that mean? It means more shit, and another success cycle will begin.

I hope by now, you see the pattern I've been laying out here, and that it will bring you peace of mind when it seems like your life is always two steps forward, one step backward. Just know that as you go through this, while the lows will always suck, the successes will get more and more significant. The other thing I want you to know, is that the graduate program you will be accepted into will be the most challenging thing you will have ever faced, but don't worry, you will figure out how to make it through, and it will become just another landmark of another success cycle. Speaking of the cycle, your future child just informed me that there is an urgent issue in the bathroom and that I need to go there immediately. I don't mind going back to the bottom, but I do wish that it could be something other than shit.

Justin

8.
Having Kids

Dear Justin,

So, you are finally ready to discuss having kids? Well, congratulations! You now understand that the closest you will ever be to "ready to have kids" is being able to think about it without having a full panic attack. It may still cause you to hyperventilate a bit, but that is normal. It is an amazing journey, and it's worth every bit of sacrifice, but it does require just that- sacrifice. Also, I am sure that you have figured out that the only way I can write this letter is because you will in fact have kids of your own. I don't want to give away too many details because the surprises are part of what causes you to grow as a person and parent, but still, I would like to share some very practical information you may find helpful.

For starters, I want you to understand that everyone experiences the moment of becoming a parent in a unique way. When your child is born, many people will ask you what it was like seeing them for the first time, expecting some beautifully poetic description of how the clouds parted and a ray of sunlight hit their face. In reality, one of your first thoughts is going to be something like "Holy shit, so this is what responsibility feels like." In addition, it really will be like meeting someone for the first time; you are excited and a little nervous to meet them, but you don't really know anything about them. I'm not sure if this is what it's like for other people, but don't worry, I don't think there is anything wrong with you. The feelings will come later. I consulted your future wife on this, and she reported having a somewhat similar experience (besides having a 7 pound 11 ounce human exit her body), but she also had thoughts such as "Hey, they just handed me a baby. It's so cute! Is it healthy? Is it normal? Oh shit, that's <u>my</u> baby."

Second, there is a ton of information out there about parenting techniques; so instead, I would like to help you with your transition from adult into parent. I will start out with some short bullet points that are very useful to know before you become a parent. Following that, I will give you some advice that I hope will ease your soon-to-be-parent mind. Here are the bullet points:

- Before your child is born, you need to channel your inner dung beetle and get your shit together. No matter what you do, your kids will become like you.

- You need to learn to be a parent, not a friend. This is a hard one because everyone wants to be best buddies with their kids. If you don't learn to be a parent to your kids, you will likely be raising your grandkids as your own children.

- It is unfortunate, but other parents and even non-parents harshly judge parents. It probably has something to do with insecurity, but just don't worry about it and do what works best for you.

- Talk to your kids like adults. I don't mean talk about adult topics, but if you speak clearly to them in the beginning, it will help them to speak back sooner.

- Never underestimate what kids are capable of understanding.

- Kids love art projects and it's good for them on many levels. However, if any of your friends or family try to give your kids glitter of any kind, you should disown them immediately. They are bad people.

Think of these bullet points as your new parent candidate starter pack. They should point you in the right direction, even if you read no further in this letter. If you choose to read, further now I would like to dig a little deeper into the details of some of these bullet points.

Good parenting will take nothing short of a heroic effort and will be the ultimate test of teamwork between you and your partner. It will most certainly transform your relationship, in some ways for the better and others for the worse, so now I would like to give you a few bits of advice, tips, and discussion points to help both of you prepare for your transition into parenthood.

1. Try to work through personal matters with your partner <u>before</u> having kids

2. Allow each parent to play to their strengths

3. Understand that male and female parents experience different kinds of stress

4. Don't die on every battlefield

That first one, working through personal matters, ensures that you both enter parenthood on a stable foundation. Both of you are going to be pushed to your limit- you will be unbelievably exhausted, the noise level in your house will probably be above OSHA (The Occupational Safety and Health Administration is a government agency that helps maintain safety for employees in the workplace.) standards, and at times it will feel like you don't even have time to take care of your own basic needs (bathing and using the bathroom). If there are any underlying issues between the two of you, they will likely come to the surface, and that's not the worst part. What's worse is that you will not have the time or the energy to work through those issues in a rational way.

Just to be clear, I'm not saying that you need to have a perfect relationship before having kids, but if you have any gaping holes in the basics such as trust, and communication, start working on them now. Having a child will not close those gaps. If anything, it will make them wider. If I had to say there was one relationship skill that was most important for both your future spouse and me to have in those early weeks, it was good communication. I am proud to say that this will be a strength of you and your wife's relationship- she will become so tired at times and will only communicate with you through basic grunts and gestures, and you will understand them.

Next, it's a good idea to discuss what your individual roles are going to be in terms of housework, meal prep, laundry, and all the others things you need to do to maintain a somewhat sane and sanitary household. Don't plan things out too tightly, because when that baby shows up, it will certainly have plans of its own requiring you to pivot a few times. The one thing that I will say is that you should at least try to let each parent focus on their strengths.

You will not have time to worry about if the chore is considered traditional or non-traditional for your gender, or what others will think of you doing that chore. If you are good at it, you just do it. If you are the master seamstress/tailor in the family, then mend the clothes. If you are the one who can crunch numbers, then balance the accounts. I'm sure you see where I'm going with this. If she can fold laundry with the precision of an automation facility, let her do it. If she can rotate tires like a NASCAR pit crew, let her do that too. My point is you won't have time or energy to waste. Just figure out who is going to do what job, traditional or not, and get that shit done.

There are of course some jobs that can only be done by a certain sex (e.g. breastfeeding) which brings me to our next topic: the different types of stress that male and female parents experience. There will be a great number of joys you will both experience when becoming parents and they will only bring you together, but understanding the different stressors will help you better support each other when times get tough. Your future wife once again allowed me to interview her about the stresses of becoming a parent, and just to put things into perspective, her physical and mental toughness is not normal. I could tell many stories about that, but nothing can top the fact that she ejected that 7 pound 11 ounce human from her body au naturale- no drugs, no nothing, just her body and her will. You can't beat that. Nonetheless, she is human, so here are some of the stresses that she experiences.

First is the obvious physical stress of pregnancy and childbirth. I'm not going to get into that because it's her story to tell, but on a rough day, she once said, "You know those magazines where pregnant women look great and say that they feel great? Well that's a bunch of BULLSHIT." She also said that going straight into breastfeeding was an unbelievable physical demand that just continued to pummel her body, and made it feel like "everyone wanted a piece of her." She once offered to show me what breastfeeding felt like and then came at my nipples with a piece of sandpaper. I respectfully declined. The physical demands of being a parent were also very disruptive to her healthy and active lifestyle, making it difficult to do the things that would normally be grounding like working out and maintaining a healthy diet.

The stress of becoming a parent was more than just physical for her. She often felt like being a mom meant she needed to be everything to everyone and often felt inadequate if she could not figure out what the baby needed right away, especially in public. As I said earlier, there are many joys of becoming a parent, but these are just some of the stressors from her perspective.

From my perspective, the stress was less physical but more mental. I'm sure you have heard the cliché that when you become a parent, you lose your identity and are only referred to as "that kid's parent." Well it was true for me. With all the attention on mom and the new baby, at times it felt like I was just disappearing into the background. In addition, if you have friends that do not have kids yet, they will be somewhat indifferent to your situation. You can't blame them; they just aren't there yet. Lastly, when you are in public with your newborn without your wife, it will occasionally feel like people expect that because you are a dad that you have absolutely no idea how to parent. Sometimes they will be right, but as I said in the bullet points, people can be very judgmental of new parents so try not to worry about what others think.

My last main point is a reminder that you will make mistakes and have "parenting fails" throughout your journey. I remember a particular morning when I had gotten up to use the bathroom and was so tired that I didn't even realize that the baby had followed me in. I was standing there taking care of business when I suddenly heard this grinding sound, and looked down to see that the baby was chewing on the toilet bowl. Definitely, a parenting fail. The good thing is that kids are very resilient, and are also forgiving. The best thing to do is to not beat yourself up over every failure (See Chapter 2: Failure) and as you know better, do better.

There is still a lot more that I could tell you about becoming a parent, but I think this is enough to start getting you prepared for this exciting and difficult challenge. Before you begin, just do a little relationship work with your partner, focus on the jobs you are good at, be mindful of each other's stress, and let go of your failures. Just know that when you become a parent, there is always more to learn and there will be more mistakes to make. Just relax and pay attention to you kids! It goes by quickly and it's actually kind of fun.

Justin

NATE'S LETTERS

9.

Reason Versus Purpose

Dear Nate,

In this first letter, I would like to focus on a phrase I have heard repeatedly: "Everything happens for a reason." Some people say this to those who are grieving or deeply struggling because it just seems like the right thing to say, but here I'm just going to give you a quick warning- don't. First, it can make the suffering individual feel as if you are minimizing their suffering. In other words, by stating everything happens for a reason, you are preventing yourself from practicing empathy and being present with the grieving person. It is a coping mechanism so that you may keep the suffering person's pain at a distance. We want suffering people to understand that there is purpose in suffering which is my second main point. Now allow me to differentiate between reason and purpose, as these are two very different concepts.

"Purpose comes from the old French word porpos, meaning 'aim or intention'. Reason from the olde French word raisoner, meaning 'to question or to challenge'. When we are arrogant and assign reasons for why certain events happen, we drown out the purpose behind those experiences. When we assign a reason to an experience we name it, challenge it and, it becomes part of who we are. **If we are able to remain quiet, and consciously aware of the tragic event, we increase our chances of being able to see the purpose behind it.** "Use purpose to aid your growth as a human being," said Dr. Zach Thomas, one of my best friends and colleagues.

There could be many reasons why something happens. Take a fender bender on the road. There are probably 50 reasons why one car stopped suddenly. Their child in the backseat may have distracted one driver, while they were running late for work. Four cars ahead another driver cut someone off, causing everyone behind them to slam on the breaks. A different driver is busy thinking about the big presentation at work tomorrow, and answering a call, and there's a loud song playing on the radio, and on, and on, and on. It all ends with that last driver hitting someone else's car, giving them a nice jolt and a good dent in the fender.

No one will argue that a fender bender is a bad thing. However, we have no idea what the ripple effects of the simple fender bender will be and what actions those drivers will take in the future. We also don't know how it may drastically affect their lives moving forward. Maybe someone will perceive it as a wakeup call to be present in his or her life. Maybe someone will start taking care of themselves to recover from the whiplash, so they begin building habits that will keep them healthy for the rest of their lives. Maybe after some time and distance, they could even look back at that simple fender bender as a gift, if they find purpose in it.

Everything has a purpose. Sometimes it's up to us to find what that purpose is and sometimes it's up to us to create that purpose. When I look for the reasons for something that already happened it keeps my vision, or my perspective locked onto the past. Moreover, it can often lead me to fall into shame, blame, or guilt. I think we can agree those are not very productive emotions long term. If, however, I can find or create purpose, I can begin to focus on healing and improving.

The best way I can illustrate this is to talk about a specific period of my life when I became depressed and suicidal. There were countless reasons why this happened. Trying to understand the reasons that led to my depression would not help me in my healing journey. Lord knows I tried to map out all the events that led to me feeling like I did. Focusing on the reasons exclusively kept me focused on the past. All the experiences became shackles to that state of depression. The only way I could fully move through and out of the state of depression was to wait for understanding of purpose through stillness.

I eventually discovered that the purpose for my depression was that now I can be with someone on their darkest days and not shrink from them. I now have deep empathy and compassion. The purpose was to understand that life is beautiful and that a brighter future is possible, and can be created.

Giving myself time and distance from the pains and struggles of my past allowed me to receive the gifts that come from pain and struggle (See Chapter 1: Struggling). Pressure can be a powerful thing. Pressure on an egg can cause it to crack or pressure can turn coal into a diamond. The pressure showed me one of my greatest sources of strength, optimism. Being an optimist is not about denying the current situation but about continually moving towards a brighter future. To quote one of my favorite movies, "Hope is a good thing, maybe the best of things, and no good thing ever dies."

Everything has a purpose. Finding the purpose in experiences...that's where the magic happens. Stephen Patton will be the first to introduce you to this idea. In addition, it will come in a high school PE class of all places. In between running the mile and rappelling down the gym walls, Patton will introduce you to mindfulness. Moreover, eventually, you'll meet someone named Dr. Wade Port who helps you live by this principle one day. He'll introduce you to living from your values instead of your unconscious needs: to live based on a vision. A little while later, you'll meet Dr. Suzan Rossi who helps you embody that trust in life. Just as Luke found Ben Kenobi to help him learn the ways of the force, these three teachers will help you learn to trust Source. Give them each a hug from me.

Purposefully yours,

Nate

10.
Fear Of
Being Wrong

Dear Nate,

In this letter, I would like you to know that YOU ARE GOING TO BE WRONG IN LIFE A GREAT DEAL AND THAT'S OK! Somewhere along the way, you like many people, have equated being correct or being perfect as factors contributing to being successful. You thought that making mistakes was a character weakness that would prevent you from being successful. Many of these ideas overlap with Justin's letter on failure, but these ideas are so important that I want to approach them from a slightly different but compatible perspective.

For starters, I would encourage you to push yourself beyond your comfort level in as many aspects of your life as you can so that you make more mistakes. Making more mistakes because you are pushing yourself to the boundaries of your current abilities means that you are growing. Make these mistakes, and be wrong and acknowledge them so you may grow. When you're wrong, become curious about it. One of the keys to a life well lived, and a life well loved, is curiosity, and this will lead you to situations where you will be wrong. That's a good thing. Staying curious allows you to constantly be in a state of awe and wonder about the world. This is the nature of science to observe and to constantly ask questions: As you go, when it turns out that you're wrong, it is not a failure. It is simply an opportunity that allows you to ask a better question: to find the blind spot in your thinking, in your beliefs, in how you interact with the world.

So often, we approach life as a series of finite games. To quote optimist and author Simon Sinek, "Life is an infinite game. People come in and out, but the game goes on." As he writes, because it is an infinite game there is no winning. It is about continuously finding the will and resources to keep playing. The most important parts of life are relationships, family, and living with purpose. Of course, there are smaller, finite games within the infinite game. You will attend many different schools throughout your education and they will seem like they will never end, yet they all end. You may have several jobs and multiple careers in your life. You will have different relationships and friendships as you go through life.

When you eventually graduate school with an advanced degree (yes it will someday happen), and you "win that game", you'll move into the infinite game of real life. As you do, don't fall for the great trap: the "Comparison Game." It is so easy to look at friends as having a better life or being better than you are. In addition, when that happens we fall into the trap of judging ourselves. "I must have the wrong approach; they must know the right way to do things." We create an illusion that we are wrong and others are right (see Paul's Chapter 21: Live Within Your Means), that is also caused by playing the comparison game).

The great shift occurs when we change the perspective from right or wrong, to being ahead or behind. Not ahead or behind other people, but ahead or behind of where we desire to be. The simple mantra can be "I'm not there yet, but I'm closer than I was yesterday."

This is why it is important to know what kind of life you want to create. Get clear on the vision you have for your life and begin working towards it.

Know that you are closer than you were yesterday. Consistency and time are the necessary ingredients for any great endeavor. Try different strategies and techniques. Ask for advice when necessary. If none of these techniques bears fruit, just know that there is always another approach out there.

This is the time to look at your friends who "have it all together", for inspiration and guidance. Just like you, they are attempting to create the best life possible. Just like you, they stumble and fall. In addition, just like them, you can get up again.

As you continue to create a life you love, it is equally important not to fall into the comparison trap of thinking you finally found the RIGHT way. This might lead you to judging yourself as superior to others. The great trap of the ego is that if you are less than someone is, and then you must be ahead of someone else. This thinking locks us into competition with each other. When in reality, no one has to lose for you to win.

The important thing is to keep moving forward and stay curious. When something doesn't work or you find you are wrong, get curious. Curiosity will lead you to ask better questions. Better questions help you find the best solutions to challenges. Curiosity helps you be in a state of awe, wonder, and allows you to have fun in life. We are all just throwing things at the wall to see what sticks. To put it more elegantly, Rumi, the 13th century Persian poet, once wrote, "Out beyond the ideas of right and wrong doing, there is a field. I'll meet you there."

I'll meet you there,

Nate

11.
Gratitude

Dear Nate,

It's going to be a rough couple of years, or at least an interesting couple of years for you, so be ready. You will struggle with a great deal, and it will feel like you're always on edge. When you enter a room, your eyes will dart around searching for who is there looking for the safety of friends or for any potential threats. Your brain will be locked in fight or flight. This is what happens when you experience so much stress that your body starts to perceive everything through the window of survival. If you want to get very nerdy about it, your sympathetic nervous system will be in a dominant state of control.

Because you're viewing the world through that lens, your body will be responding in kind. Your resting heart rate will be higher than it needs to be. Your lungs will breathe heavier than they need to, and your muscles will always seem tense. It will seem like no matter what you do, your muscles are like compressed pistons ready to fire.

What's happening is that most of the stress you've been experiencing will be stuck in the body as tension. This causes the oldest, reptilian part of the brain to be activated turning every event in your life into a survival situation. Here's the real problem; the ancient part of your brain limits the activation of the prefrontal cortex of the brain, the newest part of your brain. The prefrontal cortex is the most evolved part of the brain that houses learning, creativity, joy, and logic.

Therefore, here's what you should do to bring that prefrontal cortex back online: practice gratitude. Now just to be clear this is a gratitude PRACTICE, not an attitude. As you know (thoroughly), you can have an attitude for something without it being a practice. Like how someone (definitely not you) can have a gym bag, gym shoes, gym shorts, and a gym membership BUT not go to the gym. This would be an attitude of going to the gym, rather than a practice of it. So many people know exactly what to do to have a better life, but information isn't the key to implementation, you need to ignite action. You need to put the information into practice.

To build this practice is remarkably simple. Keep a notebook next to your bed. At the end of every day, give yourself five extra minutes to write. Write down at least three things you are grateful for that happened that day. Write in detail. Write more than three if you wish. Fill up the page.

If there is a particularly rough day, you may only be able to write that you are grateful for the day ending. If so that is ok. Write that and then come up with two more things for which you are grateful.

Use the next page to play with the practice:

1.

2.

3.

4.

Do this for three consecutive months. On average, it takes 66 days for a new habit to be formed. Give yourself the extra month to anchor the habit. During this time, your nervous system will rewire itself in a new healthier pattern. Your prefrontal cortex will become more activated. Your reptilian brain can get back to what it was meant to do running your physiology, and then you get to relax.

This will help you walk into any situation and immediately look for what is good, not what is bad or dangerous. It will help you find where the energy is at, and how it is working for you. This unbelievably simple practice can change how you interact with the world. This is what it did for me. When I first got to professional school, the president of the university recommended this practice to me. I thought to myself, "What the hell, it's not like it will hurt." Therefore, I started writing down things I was grateful for at the end of the day. After a couple weeks I felt my mood improve, my mind be more relaxed, and I actually had more energy. My body wasn't running on survival instincts anymore. This practice of being grateful is simple and powerful.

Gratefully yours,

Nate

12.
Don't Go It Alone

Dear Nate,

Paul, Justin and I have all stressed how important it is to work hard in our letters. Consistent effort over time is how you create a life you love. Now it is time for advice that is just as critical: don't go it alone. So often in this country, we hear that people need to pull themselves up by their bootstraps. I love the sentiment behind that expression. How I hear it is that everyone has the potential to rise after falling down. That is important. However, the missing part of the expression is that it is important to ask for help when you really need it, not just whenever something becomes a bit uncomfortable (see Chapter 1: Struggling).

Humans are social creatures. We are not the fastest, strongest, or most agile animals on the planet. However, we figured out how to work together. It is our greatest gift. Whether it is learning organic chemistry, starting a non-profit, or starting a country, there is so much more that we can do together.

Something magical happens when people come together for a cause and to stand for something that is beyond their own self-interest. In college, my friends and I (just wait until you meet them, they are fantastic!) were able to learn and perform academically at a high level. We worked together and helped each other learn. Whenever we had to study for long hours, our mantra became, "to one day help people, to one day help people, to one day help people." We were united in helping each other learn because we were working for something greater than ourselves. As you work, find others who have the same goals as you.

This same group of friends and I also started a non-profit in college (in case you don't know yet, nonprofits are organizations formed explicitly to benefit the public good). We all went on a service trip to Nicaragua. While in Nicaragua, it became clear that the main problem affecting people's health was contaminated water. When we returned to the States, we partnered with other groups on campus. We shared what we had seen and what we wanted to do. The professors (including Paul) who ran the trip supported us and helped us build our non-profit organization to help with the contaminated water on the Island of Ometepe, Nicaragua. This student organization continues to improve water quality in Nicaragua to this day.

The only way that this organization became successful and continues to be successful is because people trusted each other and worked hard together. Trust is built over time. To gain trust with people you must be a person of your word. Do not use your words against people and always honor the commitments you make to them. In other words, when you say you're going to do something for another person; do it. It's a simple system, but not always the easiest system to implement.

The other way you build trust is to show people that you care about them. This is as simple as remembering birthdays, asking about people's parents if you know they have a health challenge, or bringing a friend coffee when you're all studying together. Ask people real questions and listen to their answers.

Moreover, here's a great thing about working together with people; it gives you courage. Courage often comes from outside of ourselves. It comes from knowing that people around you have your back and that they love and support you. Simon Sinek, the author and motivational speaker explains, when a trapeze artist tries a new trick they have a net underneath them. The courage to try the new trick, at first, comes from knowing that the net is there to catch them if they fall. That net for most people is the support of the community. When people engage in a healing journey, having support, love, and trust in the people around them, gives them the courage to keep moving forward.

When times are tough, it is the people we trust, the people who have earned the right to be on our team, who we can lean on. One of the most powerful gestures of love and support came one day in a senior thesis class. I was so lost in my own issues that I could hardly hear what the professor (Paul) was saying. I was sitting low, elbows on my knees and head down, holding my life together with both hands and some glue. One of my best friends reached over and just put her hand on my shoulder. In that simple act, I felt better; I wasn't going through this alone.

The whole interaction lasted maybe 10 seconds. However, in it, I felt the exact support I needed. In the future when you see someone who needs help, reach out to them. In addition, when you need help, ask. We all seem to be living under this false belief that to ask for help is a sign of weakness. It is a sign of real strength. Ask for help when you need it.

As people work together for a cause and develop trust in each other, their natural gifts begin to shine. We all have gifts to share with the world. Often, these gifts are different for each of us. When you work in a group, everyone gets to share what they are good at and can be their natural best.

Is it important to work hard? Absolutely. Working hard with people is even more important. Cultivating friendships and partnerships based on trust is the most important to accomplish anything. If you want to go fast, go alone. If you want to go far, go together.

In service,

Nate

"Never doubt that a small group
of thoughtful, committed, citizens can
change the world. Indeed, it is the only
thing that ever has." - Margaret Mead

13.
Water, Water, Water

Dear Nate,

Drink more water.

Sincerely,

Nate

P.S. Ok, I realize that the introduction to this letter may have been a bit terse, so I thought I'd expand on it a bit. Before you nod politely while internally rolling your eyes, one question: how many hours over the past few years did you spend dehydrating yourself?

From the first science class you had in first grade you learned how the human body is made of mostly water. Every cell in our body requires water to function. There is a center of the brain, the hypothalamus, which keeps track of the four main biological needs. These are:

1. Are you fed?

2. Have you slept?

3. Are you well hydrated (Is there enough water in your body to function optimally)?

4. Have you continued the propagation of the human race?

Here's the best part, the hypothalamus can be tricked. When you feel tired or hungry you may actually be thirsty. If you have not slept enough or are hungry just drink water and the hypothalamus will be satisfied. Drinking water will allow you to get on with what you need to do. Drinking more water has some great benefits for when you need to be productive.

But wait there's more!

When you are dehydrated, your primitive hypothalamus does not know how to differentiate what it needs. In other words, your brain won't know if you're hungry, horny, sleepy, or thirsty.

When you're thirsty, it is incredibly easy to confuse that feeling with hunger. So if you'd like to better control your need to snack during the day, drink water.

When you are dehydrated, your brain perceives it as stress. The brain does the best thing it knows how to do when it perceives stress: it releases stress hormones. Allow me to put it another way, when you drink more water you are giving your brain another reason to feel safe, so it will be more calm and you will be more relaxed.

But wait there's more! I feel like I'm doing an infomercial for the easiest way to get healthier.

When you are well hydrated, your immune system works better, and your blood pressure will improve. If you drink more water, you will have more water in your bloodstream. If you have more water in your bloodstream, the blood is thinner, and your heart doesn't have to work as hard to pump blood through the body. Concerning the immune system, one of its main functions is to eliminate toxins from the body. More water in the body allows the kidneys to filter the blood more easily. Your body will be able to excrete waste products more often. Let me sum it up simply: When you drink more water, your body works better.

How do you get started?

The first simple guideline is that if you feel thirsty, you are dehydrated. My recommendation is to give yourself a cue to drink water throughout the day. What I began doing in professional school is to take a sip of water every time my mind wandered in class. I became the most well hydrated person on campus in no time.

Find the cue in your day, which happens often enough that it will keep you sipping water throughout the day.

And if there is ever a time that you decide you don't like the taste of water, I have one simple response: get over it and drink it anyway. It's good for you.

In conclusion, DRINK MORE WATER.

Fluidly yours,

Nate

14.
Rest

Dear Nate,

You are allowed to rest. In fact, it's highly encouraged.

The prevailing wisdom of the time is that you have to constantly be hustling one hundred percent, all day, every day, and if you are not hustling every waking minute, then you are doomed to fail.

For the record, I completely get where this comes from. Success takes time, and there are no shortcuts. Sometimes it can be accelerated, but overall it is a process, which requires time, energy, and self-discipline. You have to work hard, but there must be balance at some point either willing or unwilling (see Chapter 3: Self-Discipline).

You need to give yourself time to rest.

Sleep is the overlooked key to productivity. You will eventually understand this from your extensive study of the human body. When someone is sick all the time, can't seem to lose weight, or has no energy; the first question that needs to be asked is, how much sleep that person is getting. Give yourself time to sleep. Some basic steps to getting better sleep are to not do anything with a screen for two hours before bed, drink lots of water, and meditate before bed (Luckily, there are about 10,000 sleep meditations online.).

When you're awake, you can take time to process everything you are currently working on without the pressure of working on it. This is called giving yourself blank space. This is a time when you are not actively problem solving or working on a specific project. Your brain will be better able to connect different information when you rest then it can when you are actively thinking. To quote a friend, "Do nothing harder."

As you do important, gratifying work in life, don't forget that you need to take care of your mind and body along the way. Rather than intensity, focus on the consistency of making these changes over time. That's how people run marathons, have good dental hygiene, or build lasting relationships.

Rather than change your sleep habits all at once, be determined to make change over time. Be consistent. You will need time to rest, evaluate, and adjust. These changes are all hard to make if you feel the need to grind every day. When we're young, we want to prove our worth by trying to be the best at something. Instead, it is better to begin from a place of being secure with whom you are. It is better to live a life well lived, and come from a place where you value mastery of a skill or service to others. You want to participate in life; give yourself the time you need to rejuvenate, recover, and rest.

In loving, restful service,

Nate

15.

Shadow Dancing
In A Global Crisis

Dear Nate,

Something amazing I've learned over the last few years is called "shadow processing." It's part of why the big events in the world can feel so personal, and why sometimes-small things become overwhelming. Here's what I mean…

The Hidden Reason for Panic

Over the course of our lives, we experience some events that we cannot handle. These situations, which are too much for us to move through, cause our mind to fracture. The process of the mind fracturing is a defense mechanism. Part of us will become dissociated. In its place, we will create belief systems to protect ourselves from similar events in the future. For example, if someone's father is abusive, they may create belief systems that men are evil, or dangerous. Later in life, these belief systems will affect how we participate in our life. These "shadow" belief systems that were built from trauma or stress can affect any aspect of our lives.

Our bodies will create a physical reflection of these traumatic experiences as tension. The body is built so that all the systems are dynamically linked. Any force is instantaneously transmitted over the entire body, both at the macro level and down to the cellular level. When tension is held in the body, because of trauma, the entire body will hold the "memory" of the trauma. Every cell in our body can and often does hold onto the memory of traumatic events. Fractures of our being, trauma-based belief systems, and the "cellular memory" of the trauma all add up to "shadow": the unconscious parts of ourselves.

When current experiences are similar to old traumas, that cellular memory is activated and we experience an "echo" of the original trauma. This all adds up to create heightened chaos in our life. This will affect every part of physiology down to our DNA. Our bodies enter a sympathetically (fight or flight) dominant state. When our bodies enter that sympathetic state, we will hold abnormally high tension in the body, distorting both the large tissues and cellular structures alike. Our bodies come pre-stressed, they are built on a tensegrity structure; hard tissues suspended in a web of soft connective tissue. In other words, every part of our body is connected to all the others, and a distortion anywhere will distort the rest of the structure. Not only will it distort the muscles, tendons, and ligaments, but also it will distort through the tissues to the cellular level. This changes the function (genetic expression) of the cells. Epigenetic (non-genetic factors that affect gene expression) research is revealing what happens in one generation at a non-DNA level can affect the next two generations, and if you like the idea that our souls incarnate for multiple lifetimes, which I know you do, we can have this "shadow" from all of our lifetimes.

Part of our healing journey is to be aware of all these "shadow" components so we can deal with them. This can either be done consciously by ourselves, with the guidance of practitioners, or in community. However, this process can also happen spontaneously when life circumstances are similar enough to invite these disassociated pieces to "come home", to allow the opportunity to rewrite our belief systems, and the cellular memory. As psychologist Carl Jung wrote, "A man who is unconscious of himself acts in a blind, instinctive way and is in addition fooled by all the illusions that arise when he sees everything that he is not conscious of in himself coming to meet him from outside as projections upon his neighbor."

When a cellular memory that is disassociated "comes home", or rather "floods back" into the present lifetime reality it can often feel like it is being experienced in the present moment. If the person does not process and integrate the cellular memory, it will manifest in present reality causing disturbances, suffering, pain, and harm. As Candice Pert, Ph.D. explored in her book Molecules of Emotion, cellular chemistry will have a direct impact on our emotions, our mood, and how we think.

The beautiful advantage of this dance with our own shadow is that as we integrate these cellular memories, we let go of the trauma that created them. We get to change our previously held belief systems, and make a different choice. "I was exhilarated by the new realization that I could change the character of my life by changing my beliefs. I was instantly energized because I realized that there was a science-based path that would take me from my job as a perennial "victim" to my new position as "co-creator" of my destiny," stated by Bruce Lipton Ph.D. in his book on epigenetics The Biology of Belief.

Where We Find Ourselves

There is a disease called COVID-19 spreading across the world, caused by the sars-cov-2 virus. People have died and others continue to become ill. Now U.S. citizens are being asked to stay at home. Thousands of people have had their hours cut at work and their incomes reduced. Thousands more have been put on furlough or fired. Combined with the feelings of fear many have lived with for the past 19 years (since 9/11), this has created the perfect storm to bring up an abundance of shadow to be processed. It is entirely possible that much of the panic our society is experiencing has nothing to do with the current situation. We may be processing the cellular memory and disassociated aspects from 9/11, the Great Recession, the Great Depression, the Spanish Flu, and other pandemics humanity has experienced in the past. We have all co-created the possibility to heal centuries worth of trauma humanity has endured. It is entirely possible that we come out stronger, more loving, and more connected on the other side of this storm.

Processing and Integrating Shadow

The word enlightenment is used commonly but rarely defined. Enlightenment can be defined as when all of the disassociated pieces of self have "come home". When we have made all of the shadow aspects of ourselves conscious, they no longer control us. This journey should be accomplished safely, gently, and easily. According to healer and teacher Dennis Adams there are three key things to do to attain enlightenment, and three things to do when we are processing shadow. They are:

1. Don't judge it.

2. Don't take it personally.

3. Stay in Present Time.

Don't Judge It

This step is possibly the most challenging when we are first aware of our healing. We live in a culture that promotes self-judgement. Therefore, developing the ability not to judge your shadow as right or wrong is critical. Simply allow it to be. It's not good nor bad. The mantra I use is "That's interesting." This allows me to stay aware of it without having to determine whether it falls on the good or bad side of duality.

Don't Take It Personally

Imagine you have been doing laundry and putting clothes away in your closet. Then you come across that itchy sweater, the one a great aunt gave you that is so uncomfortable, and then you decide to put it on and feel how itchy it is. That is what taking it personally is like. When you consciously stay detached, you simply hang the sweater up and put it away. When you are processing shadow, stay unattached to the process as best as possible. Simply allow it to flow.

Stay in Present Time

When shadow comes up for processing it can pull us out of the present time. Memories of the past will begin flooding our mind faster than we can keep up with, and we will become lost in a specific event, or we will start uncontrollably visualizing the future (usually all the negative possibilities that exist). This will often present with feelings of cold hands, sweating, heavy breathing, and a fast heart rate. Thoughts will become lodged in either the past or rapidly thinking about the future. There are two simple strategies to employ when this happens. One is to gently squeeze your glute muscles. This will help "pull" you more fully into your body. Whilst doing this, the other strategy is to look around the environment you're in and name things. Begin naming things aloud to yourself.

"That blue lamp."

"The door knob."

Do this repeatedly. You will likely feel yourself calm down.

Clear the Nervous System

For centuries, different cultures around the world have acknowledged that the nervous system is the key to enhancing human consciousness. "Enlightenment is the normal, natural state of health for the body and mind.

It results from the full development of consciousness and depends upon the harmonious functioning (homeostasis) of every part of the body and nervous system. When one is using the full potential of the mind and body in this way, every thought and action is spontaneously correct and life supporting. This is life free from suffering, life lived in its full stature and significance," according to Maharishi Mahesh Yogi, developer of Transcendental Meditation.

By improving the function of the nervous system, the body is allowed to process the shadow, stress, and trauma. The chemistry of the body may shift to one of calm (parasympathetic activation), rather than being locked in fear (stress hormones and sympathetic activation). Eventually we will be better able to move, and our future generations can grow and thrive as they were meant to. As Sue Brown, D.C. often stated, "we can all take a small step on our path of evolution."

Moving Through This Time of Uncertainty

None of us knows what tomorrow will bring; however, right now this is how life is. We are all given an opportunity to remember that the only constant is change. This certainty comes from the finite perspective of our personality. Clarity is a value which all of us can embrace as we process, integrate, heal, and improve. This situation can be an opportunity to remember what is truly important to each of us, and might help us find clarity on who we are and where we choose to go after this storm passes. Moreover, since you are reading, you have a perfect record of making it through storms.

May you gracefully, easily, safely, and gently process and integrate the shadow that is coming up for you right now. May you stay in present time, stay consciously detached, and allow the shadow to flow. May you remember that **YOU ARE ENOUGH.**

See you in the future,

Nate

16.
Magic In
Your Body

Dear Nate,

Your ability to heal and be healthy is great. This ability is far greater than you've ever been led to believe. The vast majority of people view the body as a vehicle that will break down over time, and by the end of life, it will be barely chugging along. I have a different view of things. Your body and your life is meant to be like a candle, shine brightly throughout its time here, flicker a little at the very end, and then go out. There's something much more complicated, and much more magical at work with the human body.

So first thing's first, what does it mean to be healthy? If I were to ask you: "What is health?" What would you say?

Most people would say:

- "Health is feeling good."

- "Health is not having to take any medications."

- "Health is not having to go to the doctor."

Alternatively, if I ask how you know you are healthy, most will answer:

- "Well, I exercise a lot"

- "I buy my food at a health food store."

- "I feel pretty good."

I suppose the real question is where does health and healing come from, inside of you or outside of you.

Many people think they can go buy health from a health food store, a gym, or a doctor. The truth is none of those things creates health. None of those things is the source of health. Health is "a state of optimal physical, mental and social well-being and not merely the absence of disease and infirmity."

Many people say: "I am healthy. I feel good. I exercise." However, you've read about athletes, in incredible shape, who all of a sudden drop dead of a heart attack. You also know exactly what it's like to be told someone you love has cancer. The first thing you, and everyone usually feels is shock. It comes out of nowhere because you thought the person was "healthy".

You don't need to look any further than your uncle. He was told that he had late stage cancer even though he did "all the right things" to stay "healthy". However, it takes years for the cancer like he had to develop. He wasn't healthy; he just didn't have any symptoms.

In general, we're not good at measuring health. There is no machine that can indicate you're 50% healthy or you're 80% healthy. There is no x-ray, CAT scan, dog scan, or any scan that you can use that tells you how healthy you are. The best some of our medical tests can do is measure a few markers in the body that tell you how sick you are or how sick you're not. So how do we make sense of this? Remember number lines when we were in school? I'm going to create a number line, really a function line.

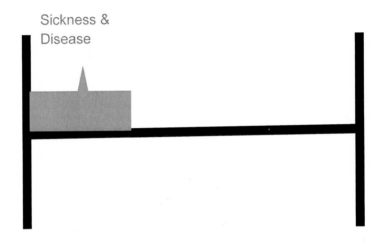

At 0% function, nothing is working in your body, or in other words, you die. One hundred percent perfect function is optimal physical, emotional, mental, spiritual, and social well-being. Optimal well-being on every level is total health. It's safe to say we live somewhere on this spectrum between 0% function (death) and 100% function (total health).

Someone with cancer is closer to the left end of the function line than to the right. Someone with high blood pressure is closer to the left than the right. Someone with back pain is closer to 0% than 100% function (health). They are all in that shaded area of reduced function on the function line that we call sickness & disease.

Most people spend most of their time trying to stay out of the sickness zone. The majority of people are completely reactive, only taking action when they experience a symptom, ache, or pain. That action is typically going to a doctor or the pharmacy aisle of the grocery store. Very often though, the person never truly moves out of the sickness zone, because the FUNCTION of your body hasn't changed. Most of the treatments for disease or dysfunction are designed to make you feel better, without improving how your body operates.

If you want to be healthier tomorrow than you are today, you need to do something to allow your body to FUNCTION better (See Paul's Chapter 26: How to Get Strong). Therefore, whatever allows your body to FUNCTION better will move you closer to total health. When the body functions better, it adapts better. When the body functions and adapts better, you get to live a sweeter life, and the best part is, the body was designed to function at a high level.

The human body is magnificent. There is a genius inside your body that knows how to heal you, create health and allow your body to function at its true potential. Most peoples' bodies make every chemical it will need in life. One of the most miraculous things the body does is heal itself. If I cut myself, - what happens? I start bleeding; I wash it off, and probably put a Band-Aid on it. Does the Band-Aid heal me? No!

Life is what heals. Life is the only healer there is. Life inside you and me is the magical force that allows our bodies to work; it's the force that allows our bodies to function. Let's say that you broke your arm. I could take you to the best hospital in the world with the most renowned doctors on Earth. They would take some x-rays to find out where the break occurred. Then they would line the bones up and put the arm in a cast. The doctors would trust the body to heal itself, to grow completely new bone, blood vessels, and nerves.

"The wisdom of the body is responsible for 90% of the hope of patients to recover. The body has a super wisdom that is in favor of life, rather than death. This is the power we depend on for life. All doctors are

responsible for letting their patients know of this great force working within them." - Dr. Richard Cabot, Harvard Medical School

Life uses the nervous system to coordinate and learn. Your brain is an electrical supercomputer more complicated than any computer humanity has ever created. Your nervous system continues from your brain down your spinal cord, a delicate cable system surrounded by bone. The wires of your nervous system connect to every tissue. Your nervous system is an electrical network, moving energy through your body and creating the chemical state you live in. This can be either a state of stress, survival, and chaos; or a state of learning, growth, healing, and adaptation.

Throughout life, things become stressful. Traumas and injuries occur, often starting as early as the birth process. Life can become overwhelming. When this happens, whatever we can't handle will become stored in the body (See Chapter 15: Shadow Dancing in a Global Crisis). Our body enters a state of chaos; we start operating from our ancient or so-called, "lizard-brain". Our nervous system becomes focused on survival. We become desensitized to our body, and to our life. Tension begins twisting, pulling, or torqueing our body into inefficient shapes. In short, we become disconnected from our bodies and from our life.

To improve the function of our body, and improve our experience of life, we need to improve the function of the nervous system. Any interference to the nervous system interferes with life working within us. We experience our entire existence through the nervous system. The better the function of the nervous system, the more freedom and joy we experience in our life. We have the mechanisms within us to improve the function of the nervous system.

Breath is the easiest of the mechanisms to improve the nervous system. You've already been breathing for years and you do it unconsciously. Have you ever noticed when you are stressed your breath is more shallow and faster. Under these conditions, only your upper chest will move in the breath and not your entire thorax. Harnessing your breath by breathing in 360 degrees around your body from the top of your chest to the bottom of your belly will not only help you relax, but help you center yourself. Breath work has been used for centuries to change physiology. There are hundreds of classes and techniques out there. As you read this, pause for a moment. Lay on your either back or lean back in your chair. Place both hands, overlapping, over the belly button. Breathe deeply in through your nose, pulling the breath into the belly so it moves your hands. Exhale out the mouth. Do this for 3 minutes...Feel a change? As you continue to use your breath consciously, you can easily shift your nervous system anywhere, anytime. It becomes easier and easier to improve function.

Our bodies crave **movement**. In fact, there is a name when all movement has stopped in the body, death. From the time, we are infants, we learn through movement. When babies are on their tummy and learn to cross-crawl, that is what wires their left and right brains together. Paul writes beautifully, later about using movement (with an external resistance) to get stronger. What is key is to move every day. The simple strategy to start this is to go for a 30-minute walk every day. It improves the function of your heart, your lungs, and the big muscle groups. It's a simple and easy way to create more function in the body.

Above all, we need more **connection**. Our culture has the most anxious, depressed, disconnected, and medicated adults in history. We are seeing more and more children suffer from the same issues. Humans need connection. This is both connection to other people through meaningful relationships and internal connection with ourselves. The most efficient and consistent way that I have found to improve the nervous system is through vitalistic chiropractic. Vitalistic Chiropractic clears these layers of trauma and stress from our nervous system. By adjusting the body, and improving the function of the spine and nervous system, you can be the best version of yourself: physically, mentally, emotionally and spiritually. The more clearly your nervous system, the more function you have in your body. Pairing this with movement and breath work allows you to rapidly accelerate your healing journey and create the healthier future you deserve.

You have all the tools inside of you to improve your life. It takes time and consistency. It takes some effort. Living a healthy life, being able to trust your body, and experiencing the magic of your body is your birthright. The same force of Life that sparked you into existence in the womb is still present in you, waiting to be unleashed. It's waiting to awaken you to how amazing life can be.

In service,

Nate

17.
Life Is
Cumulative

Dear Nate,

Nothing you have ever done has been wasted. When I was in high school English and History, I had fun, because these subjects were easy for me. It was all about learning stories; the story of what happened, what drove people, and how one action related with others.

This love of stories came from growing up and loving action figures. Some kids were into Legos or hot wheels, but we were into action figures because we loved creating our own stories. Coming up with a story and then pretending to live the story was always exciting to me.

Then when I got to college, it was sciences classes galore. I remember thinking about how it seemed like we had an uphill battle. My classes were based exclusively on data and logic. How on Earth would the "story skillset" ever apply here?

The answer became so obvious it almost slapped me in the face; look at science as a story. Treat every part of the body as a character. How do they interact and work together? How do they begin to build a community together? The brain and heart became the selfish characters who do anything to maintain their existence.

The other beautiful thing that happens when you look at biology or any science this way, is that it becomes easier to explain to people. Most people in the world don't think in terms of ion channels, data sets, statistics, or equations. Stories are how we communicate. Stories are what hold societies together. Even the United States is a shared story. One day, when you begin serving people this will become even clearer. Listen to their story. Really listen to how their lives are being affected, what are their challenges, and what do they deeply desire. Then you can help them, not because of how amazing you are, but because you know how to facilitate their healing journey. Patients ultimately get to be the heroes of their own story. It's all about helping them write a new ending to their stories.

Most importantly, be naturally curious and enthusiastic about things you love, or put another way; be a nerd. As I've moved through life, I've noticed something interesting. In junior high school, it almost seemed like being a nerd was something to be hidden. In high school, it got to be a little more acceptable. In college, being a nerd was something completely normal. By the time professional school rolled around, being a nerd was required for success. The seemingly random interests will eventually become truly useful.

Your interests will change, and they should with time. Nevertheless, continue to approach life with curiosity and enthusiasm. Let yourself become obsessed with what you love. Then something magical occurs. You get to live in that place of joy, enthusiasm, and curiosity for life.

The beauty of life is that it allows you to express who you are and who you want to be. My opinion is that we all have gifts to share on this journey we call life. Let yourself enthusiastically run towards what is drawing your attention. Someday, you'll find it was all there for a purpose (see Chapter 9: Reason Versus Purpose.). Your study of martial arts taught you how to channel movement, focus, and energy through your body. Photography helped you understand positioning, light, and timing. Even Little League showed you how fun it is to be on a team.

Each of these interests can reveal your talents and skills. You will find a specific road to travel. When you do, bring forth every aspect of who you are. As Lin-Manuel Miranda (The playwright and actor from Hamilton) stated when asked how he became so successful, he said, "Pick a lane and run as fast as you can."

Life is cumulative. Everything about who you are and what you love is important. It is all useful. Trust that your unique path will reveal itself in time. In addition, when it does, run!

Enthusiastically yours,

Nate

PAUL'S LETTERS

18.
Think Like the Successful Child of Immigrants

Dear Paul,

I am writing to you from the future. I decided to write you a series of letters to help you develop into a productive citizen. Now your idea of productivity is eating a second bowl of pasta for dinner. You have a number of supposed "advantages in life," and the primary advantage is the fortune of being born into a family of two immigrant parents. I know what you are thinking right now. You are saying to yourself, "being the eldest son of two immigrants makes me superman?" Let me explain.

Your mother is a seamstress who works at home as a housewife and your dad owns his own small business driving around in a stepvan (a van that looks like a small Federal Express truck) six days per week from 6 am-7 pm for nine months a year sharpening knives, scissors, lawn and gardening tools. He is unemployed for three months every year due to the nature of his business. By the way, he never collects unemployment when he is out of work and we never ask for handouts from anyone. I am aware that you know all of this, but it is necessary to restate the obvious for the purpose of this letter. As a young child, you have the privilege of helping your parents in the Italian vegetable garden (Some people call this garden a small farm.) on the weekends. It's not that you never get to play as a child, but simply put, your parents have different traditions and priorities than other parents. You are also taught how to fix almost everything that breaks. No piece of junk is ever truly unusable or unfixable. Your dad always does the vehicle maintenance utilizing you and your brother as assistant mechanics. By assistant mechanics, I mean that you hold a flashlight on cold dark evenings and hand your father tools. You and your brother are what I like to call "the tool boys." You also have to help your parents when they deal with doctors, bankers, and contractors. Now remember your parents are smart, but English is their second language. When playing translator for your parents, you don't have enough life experience to know if the aforementioned people are deceiving you and your parents. You are a kid, but you are forced to do adult tasks earlier than your friends do.

At this moment you are thinking, thanks for motivating me and making feel like, @#$%&*. Okay, so here's the deal. To frame this a little differently, you grow up earlier than most of your peers and this is the real advantage. Your ability to deal with setbacks and uncertainty has been forged in the fire of life. You know how to plan, but do not freak out when a plan falls apart. Why? **Nothing in your life ever goes as planned.** You understand how to make the most of scarce resources and how to make old equipment live on long after most people would have discarded it. Hard Work is the only type of work you know. Easy work sounds like some fictional nirvana that can only be conjured up by wizards, witches, and elves. You develop relationships with people who have skills that complement your own in order to survive and thrive. This is just normal living to you. Your family has a life philosophy that states that as long as you all have your health, a roof over your heads, can pay your bills, and can enjoy time with family and friends, life is great.

You don't understand why people need expensive things. That shit eventually breaks just like the inexpensive stuff, but costs big bucks to replace. At least the junky stuff you own can be easily maintained and lasts at least as long as all that expensive stuff. Don't get me wrong, the expensive stuff is cool, and someday you would like to own some of it, but you realize that the expensive cars and gadgets are simply not practical for you to buy and maintain at your age and with your resources.

Therefore, now that I have your attention, let me lay out the seven advantages or superpowers you have as the son of immigrants:

1. You have no choice but to **make more good decisions than bad** to survive and succeed.

2. You are not easily offended; **you are not "thin skinned."**

3. You **live within your means**, to survive because no one can bail-you-out if you overspend.

4. You learn to **chase contentment not happiness.**

5. You are not a remarkable person and have to **"work hard,"** at everything you do to succeed. Your parents model this way of life for you and your brother.

6. You don't like to read as a child, but soon learn that **reading frequently** allows you to sharpen your mind and enables you to excel academically, so you read often.

Finally, you realize at a young age that **respect is earned** and not given to anybody. You get your ass handed to you a few times along the way in life, but eventually learn how to earn people's respect.

Therefore, in conclusion, being the son of immigrant parents essentially teaches you lessons that most people don't learn until early adulthood, if at all. Never forget how to think like an immigrant. Hold your head up high and never ever feel like you got a raw deal in life. You are not a victim. You are one of the luckiest people on the planet for being born in the U.S. to two loving, hard working parents. They love you and teach you Judeo-Christian values. I will be writing letters to you in the near future that explain all of these "so called" advantages.

Remember the love,

Paul

19.

Make More Good Decisions Than Bad Decisions For A Successful Life

Dear Paul,

This letter describes your first immigrant advantage. This first super-power is based on a simple idea; if **you make more good decisions in your life than bad, you will succeed.** This might seem obvious, but believe me it is not to most people. Most people always look for the complicated paths to success, and overlook the obvious. Most people are looking for "life hacks" also called shortcuts to success. By a successful life, I mean a life that includes graduating high school, getting married, having some kids, making your community a better place, and of course staying out of jail. Look, nobody is perfect and what I have outlined might not be everyone's idea of a successful life, but it is for me. Along the way in life, I have made **some bad decisions, and some of those bad decisions are so bad that they could qualify me for my own reality T.V. Show. However, all of the bad decisions I have made in life I own, and in part the lessons I have learned from these bad decisions have allowed me to succeed.**

I have failed epically in school in every grade up to and including my college years. I have wasted money on a car in order to make it look like a Ferrari, but guess what, it was still a Nissan Sentra, so it turns out you can't polish a turd. I have hung out with people who did some idiotic things. Once on spring break in a Daytona Beach, Florida nightclub with three of my friends from college, one of my not so bright friends decided it would be great to smuggle a beer out the back of the club. This story sounds so idiotic; you are saying to yourself, no one could be that stupid. Oh, but indeed we were that stupid. So let me paint the picture of the series of bad decisions that occurred in Daytona, Florida on that spring break. First, of course I was <u>not</u> engaged in under-age drinking. <u>No one is allowed to carry alcohol on Daytona's streets during spring break.</u> This piece of information becomes important in a bit. Second, I am sure that the mob owned this club based on the look of the bouncer and the club manager. Third, my buddies and I decided to smuggle a cheap beer out of the club. Let me repeat that, my buddies and I decided to smuggle a cheap beer out of the club. We decided to run through the back hallway that led to the management offices, which eventually connected to the back door of the club where we ran into a fenced-in-lot full of expensive cars. I am sure all the expensive cars were stolen. In addition, my three "brilliant friends", and I then jumped the barbed-wire fence and walked past three sets of cops, on the three mile walk back to our hotel, all while my buddy carried "the beer" under his arm inside his jacket. Now let me do a wrap up analysis of the different levels of foolishness I have just finished describing. One, my friend bought the beer legally and could have simply drank it at the night-club. He had already drunk other beers and was, "Winning." Two, I was not drinking at the nightclub and could not have cared less about alcohol. I was happy just being on spring break in Daytona. I should have walked out the front door of the nightclub and met my "Brain Surgeon" friends back at the hotel. Why would I listen to people dumber than me? This is one of those eternal questions that only the Almighty can answer. Three, all of us risked being caught by the mob nightclub owner, the police, and skewering ourselves on a barbed-wire fence. We did all of this to be able to make the claim that one of us drank a cheap beer in Daytona in our hotel room on spring break. I think that of all of the potentially bad outcomes that could have occurred during this incident, being skewered by a barbed-wire fence was the lesser of all the evils. SAD!

What's the point of telling you all of this? Well, first, the story is entertaining. Second and most importantly, all of these bad decisions or "learning experiences", as I like to call them have taught me how to make good decisions. Yet with all of the bad decisions I have made, I have made even more good decisions. These good decisions include, moving to Indiana to attend the Human Performance Laboratory at Ball State University to earn a Master's in Exercise Physiology. There I met this wonderful woman from Milwaukee, Wisconsin and married her. I decided to sharpen my intellect and become an excellent scientist by spending four and a half years working as the head technician in my future doctoral mentor's laboratory, so that when I applied to a Ph.D. program, I would be a stronger candidate. In addition, I decided to start saving for my retirement in my mid-twenties. I decided on many occasions to put my ego aside and not break people's faces by getting into fights. This kept me out of jail, and not having a criminal record goes a long way to helping me become successful.

In conclusion, by making more good decisions than bad, and by learning a great many lessons from my bad decisions, even if some of those bad decisions almost make me a candidate for the Darwin Awards, I ultimately, succeed. By the way, "The Darwin Awards salute the improvement of the human genome by honoring those who accidentally remove themselves from it in a spectacular fashion!" Regardless of all my spectacular fails, I have carved out the exact version of a good life I envisioned. Ultimately, I have become a better, more compassionate person, and can now look back at all this lunacy and laugh. The success I have achieved is not bad for a person who has made so many epic mistakes in life, and who is otherwise unremarkable.

Remember the Love,

Paul

20.
Don't Be
Thin Skinned

Dear Paul,

I am writing to you today to ask you not to be thin skinned, and don't be easily offended. Humans, the same species that invented the Darwin Awards, have become crippled by trying to never offend anyone. Most people desire to treat our fellow man with kindness. I agree with this notion, but taken to its extreme, this notion has the potential to create anxiety. Unless you never have your own opinion on any topic, you will eventually offend someone. The best term to describe these phenomena is political correctness. Political correctness is a term used to describe language that is intended to avoid offense to members of particular groups in society. While I agree with the intention of this term, society has taken this political correctness too far.

To clarify, no one wants you to be a complete asshat, but being alive means you need to learn to live with people being rude, insensitive, mean, nasty, and caustic. The sooner you can start to ignore negative language, the sooner you can actually help the world be a better place. The cliché, "Sticks and stones will break your bones, but words can never hurt you" applies here.

You are a human being who has the choice to be or not to be offended. Just choose to ignore jerks and move on.

This reminds me of a story of a bully I encountered in the 8th grade. This kid, whom I will refer to as "Mongo," had a locker next to mine for the entire year. He was four inches taller than I was and outweighed me by at least 40 pounds. Every school day morning he greeted me at my locker with a smile and some smart-ass remark, and then he slammed my locker shut. This went on until April and I was becoming more-and-more upset with him as time passed. At this point in my life, I was "thin skinned." The thing is that he is not the biggest jerk I have ever met in my life, but this person hurt my feelings every day. One day I decided to turn the tables on Mongo and make a put-down comment about myself before he could say a word, and then I slammed my own locker before Mongo could. Mongo and I both laughed, and became friends for the rest of the year. I stopped being thin skinned and angry all the time. From then on, when people insulted me or called me a dweeb, nerd, geek, or jerk, I looked at them with a smile and laughed. By being "thick skinned", some of the other jackasses I met in life also became my friends. If you can't laugh at yourself, it might be because you are thin skinned.

Remember that hateful words are not the same as someone pointing a gun at your head. Barack Obama, a future President of the United States makes a statement at the end of his second term in office that goes something like this, "if you are always looking to be offended, you always will be offended." Get over yourself and develop thick skin, and try to find humor in words, because at the end of the day, they are just words.

Remember the love,

Paul

21.
Live Within
Your Means

Dear Paul,

Hello again and just in case you are counting, this is my fourth letter to you, on my mission to help prevent you from becoming a waste-of-life. In the United States of America, many people are living beyond their means. Why is this a problem? This is a problem, because there is a lack of balance, and as a physiologist, I can attest that humans need balance. Let me recount a story that one of my accounting professors told me that highlights what happens when people don't live within their means. He once had a client who worked in the finance industry and owned expensive cars, houses, and other toys. In addition, this client would take multiple expensive vacations every year. So far this sounds like a person who makes a great deal of money and who is not afraid to spend it. You think to yourself, this is no big deal, dude. You might also be thinking that you would love to be this person. Fair enough. Here is the rub; this client was making about $250,000.00 per year. Again, you are thinking to yourself, this is cool, and I would concur. This same client however, had also accumulated over $100,000.00 in credit card debt, not so cool. The point of the story is no matter how much you make, you still need a budget and need to live within your means. If you are smart enough and work hard, enough to make $250,000.00 per year then please do not act as if you have a brain that has only two functional neurons (brain cells). Spend money like a responsible adult. I know the word adult is scary, but get over it. If you make $30,000.00 per year or even $1,000,000.00 per year, you need to spend less than you make. The math is about as simple as it gets. It is okay to dream about having nice expensive stuff, but you need to be able to afford the nice expensive stuff. I have a method of being frugal that I like to refer to as, "running things into the ground." You might call me a cheap-ass, but I call it "non-wasteful."

I used the running things into the ground technique with my first new car. This car was a Nissan Sentra; remember the pseudo-Ferrari? The only extra I purchased with this car was air conditioning. There was no radio. This same car only had a driver's side mirror and partial steering assist. By partial steering assist, I mean I built some superhero strong arms just from trying to turn that thing. Whenever I would turn the steering wheel in a tight parking lot to get into a parking space, I would be out of breath. I owned this car for 12 years and put 134,000 miles on it. I maintained it to the best of my ability, but eventually I felt the need to get it checked out by a mechanic. He inspected the car and told me that one day when driving to work, the rear wheels would make it to work before the rest of the car. This car was such a junk heap at this point that when I tried to trade it in when purchasing a new car, the mechanic from the dealership laughed at me and said, "I will do you a favor and take this junk heap off your hands." I know this makes me sound like a miser, but I was smart enough to know that the car was at the end of its useful life, because I always run things into the ground. What using this technique does for me is it allows me to save for retirement and my children's' college tuition. Play the long game and delay gratification in all parts of your life, and it will pay off. Live within your means.

Remember the love,

Paul

22.
Chase Contentment, Not Happiness

Dear Paul,

Ciao (hello)! Many people talk about living a happy life or just simply wanting to be happy. I am here to tell you that happiness is great but it doesn't always last, so when you are happy, appreciate it. In addition, some people are never happy, and no one wants to be around these miserable humans. That being said, it is almost impossible to walk around always being happy. Some people are good at faking it, especially on social media, but that is a rant for a future letter. Humans feel a spectrum of emotions and happiness is only one of those many emotions. Simply put, happiness is fleeting, and so you have to be able to function most of your life in spite of not being in a constant state of happiness. This doesn't mean that you are always sad, anxious, or depressed either, but that something else must power what you do, and that energy source must be a sense appreciating what you already have- this is called being content.

So how did I learn about being content? Well, life teaches you many things, but I can trace this philosophy back to my parents and many of their immigrant friends. All of these people including my parents always seemed happy to me. It was difficult for me to reconcile how all of these people worked extremely hard every day and owned very little and still they seemed happier than people who had fancier houses, cars, and just fancier stuff in general. The Oxford Dictionary defines happiness as, "the state of pleasurable content of mind, which results from success or the attainment of what is considered good." This was not quite the word to describe my parent's state of being. It was not that my parents and their friends were always happy, but they were content. The Oxford Dictionary defines contentment as, "having one's desire bound by what one has (though that may be less than one could have wished).

My parents were satisfied with what they owned and mostly they were satisfied with all of the relationships they had with friends, family, and neighbors. My parents were always singing and getting excited about mundane events like traditional Italian Sunday dinner. Let me paint the picture of a traditional Italian Sunday dinner. This is the largest most indulgent meal of the week of a typical immigrant Italian family. For this meal, my mother would always set the large fancy table in the traditional dining room. Many times, we would have friends over to enjoy the meal with us. The table would have a beautifully woven imported tablecloth with cloth napkins and real silverware. This meal consisted of five to seven courses starting with a course of antipasto (an appetizer such as olives, dry sausage, and cheese), and followed by pasta, of course. Course three always had at least two to three types of meat such as meatballs, braciola (This is a type of rolled up meat stuffed with salt, pepper, Romano cheese, parsley, and raisins tied with string.) and some type of cooked sausage. Usually following the meat course would be the salad, which was then followed by a course of nuts and fruit. Obviously, there was always wine served with this dinner. Finally, we would have a dessert with espresso coffee. Eating on Sunday would take hours, but we loved the great conversation and being with family and friends. Writing about this traditional meal makes me hungry, content, and happy.

In the end, I learned that I would be happy sometimes, but that I should always be content. This does not mean to stop having goals or striving to be better, but along the way be content in that moment with who you are and what you already have. If these poor people like my parents and their friends who had so little could be content and enjoy life's simple pleasures, then so could I. To this day, I remember my mother's words of wisdom: "Always be content with what you have, but also appreciate happiness when it comes." Life is too short not to appreciate the simple blessings of life.

Remember the Love,

Paul

23.
Work Hard

Dear Paul,

Ciao bello! That is Italian for hello beautiful, but you know that. Lesson number five as we travel down the road of making you less of a meathead, highlights the immigrant superpower of working hard. Believe it or not, some people think you only need to work smarter, not harder. I agree that working smarter increases your efficiency, but if you have not built a foundation of hard work, then what are you trying to make more efficient? Recently, we as a society have been giving out trophies to all participants in sports. Everyone's children apparently are above average at everything and no one needs to work hard. Yeah sure, everyone is above average, and I am going to be starring in the next Marvel's Avengers movie. These people do not understand simple statistics. Believe it or not, not everyone is working hard at life. Working hard is pushing yourself beyond your current barriers. A former colleague of mine required students to study two to three hours for every hour that they were in her cellular and molecular biology class lecture; students needed to study 14-21 hours per week for her class before they were allowed to approach the professor to complain that the test was unfair. In other words, these students first needed to be working hard, before they were allowed to complain.

Let us look at Elon Musk as a role model for hard work. Elon Musk is a billionaire immigrant originally from Pretoria, South Africa who started some of the most groundbreaking companies in the last 20 years, including PayPal. He is currently involved in SpaceX, Tesla, Neuralink, Hyperloop, and the Boring Company. Musk's I.Q. I would guess places him in the near-genius category and yet he always talks about working 80-120 hours per week. Remember a full workweek for most Americans is between 40 and 50 hours per week. Elon with all his intellectual gifts still works two to three times as much as the average American. He works hard.

I personally succeed in academics, in my career, in my marriage, and in my friendships through hard work. I realize that I must embrace "the suck." Hard work is foundational to all success. The following story exemplifies this best. In order to enter a Ph.D. program, I take the graduate record exam (GRE) three times and score terribly on the math, logic, and the verbal sections the first two times. By the way, the GRE is the standardized exam used by most Ph.D. programs for admissions purposes. Basically, I scored at the "amoeba level" on the exam (an amoeba is a single celled organism that does not have a brain). So what do I do to be less like an amoeba? I talk to some truly smart people and they give me some hints and encourage me on how to succeed on the GRE. I spend the next six months learning over 1,000 new vocabulary words and memorizing basic math rules and practicing logic problems. When I take the GRE for the final time, I score excellent on the math and the logic sections of the exam, but I destroy the verbal section of the exam and score in the 97 percentile. The score is so high that when I interview for a Ph.D. position for graduate school, one of the faculty members says that she has never seen a 57-percentile increase in any GRE score. She asks me what my secret is, and I tell her that I worked "really" hard. She laughed at me and said, "Sure you did." She mentioned to me that she thought I had "smart-kid syndrome." This is a condition where smart people are lazy and underperform out of sheer laziness. In her mind this was the reason for my first two fails on the GRE. I reassured her that I was just an average guy, who worked hard. She shook her head and we continued with the interview.

Here is the deal. The beauty of living in a country like the United States of America is that everyone gets to choose how hard they want to work. Don't ever be jealous of someone else's success if they worked their butts off. Celebrate others' successes and if you want what they have achieved then start working hard doing all the things that someone must do in order to succeed. Every strong house is built on a strong foundation. The stronger the foundation, the larger the house you can build. Hard work is foundational, and when optimized will allow you to build strong relationships and a career. Work hard my friend, as it will serve you well for the rest of your life.

Remember the love,

Paul

24.
Read Often

Dear Paul,

What is up? Today's letter from your future self focuses on immigrant advantage six. Something you are going to find extremely (insert sarcasm) exciting: reading. This one is not exclusively an immigrant advantage, but it is an important lesson that you learn from your mother who is an immigrant. This activity changes you for the rest of your life. I know what you are thinking, with all of the advice that you could give me from the future, you want to talk to me about something that I do not currently enjoy. In case you have not figured it out yet, these letters are not meant to entertain you. These letters are like eating your vegetables; they are something you need in order to develop.

Why reading? Reading is a foundational skill from which many other important skills are built. Reading first teaches patience. It takes patience to read a 300-page book. It teaches you to delay gratification by having to wait days or even weeks to get to the end of a great murder mystery book to find out who did it. Reading teaches you how to pay attention for extended periods. Being able to focus for long periods in the early 21st century will be almost impossible with all of the distractions that humans will encounter.

Nonetheless, having a longer attention span will allow you to learn more and hopefully be more efficient with your learning.

You will also develop a larger vocabulary by being exposed to many more words than you might encounter in casual conversation. Do not underestimate the importance of your ability to use the English language for your success. Take this advice from a person whose first language was Italian and not English. You will also become a better writer at first simply because you will have a larger vocabulary and because you will be able to mimic the styles of writers whose books you read. This effect is similar to how you mimicked your parents when you learned to speak.

Reading books, helps train your attention span. Reading will also allow you to have the greatest minds in every field of human endeavor that have ever lived to be your mentors. People like Mother Theresa, Marcus Aurelius, Margaret Thatcher, Golda Meir, Richard Feynman, Dwight D. Eisenhower, Nelson Mandela, and Winston Churchill will be your greatest teachers. Most people are lucky to have two fine mentors in their parents, and maybe a friend or boss, but to have an unlimited number of mentors, from any field, is simply amazing.

Even reading fiction, science fiction, science fiction-fantasy will pay huge dividends. You will be able to be whisked off to never before imagined lands populated by fantastical creatures and beings. Your imagination will grow immensely. Many of today's greatest inventions and breakthroughs began as part of someone's imagination. In addition, you will learn that reading will serve as a type of meditative practice where the rest of the world melts away for a short period and your mind can rejuvenate itself. In that same vein, reading teaches you to become comfortable with your own thoughts and being alone (This being alone thing will eventually be covered in a future book.). As long as you have a book, you are never truly alone. Also, I would like to point out that your mother, who did not even have a high school education, was reading all the time. She was setting the example for me. She was a very bright woman, and maybe reading had something to do with it. As I think back, many of your mother's Italian-born friends read quite a bit. I don't think that's a coincidence.

If you add up all of the benefits that I have discussed so far, they would make reading worthwhile. In addition, the foundation that reading creates for your mind and soul will allow you to build other skills, so-called Meta skills. Meta skills is a topic for another day, but in short, Meta skills are higher order skills that allow a person to use and integrate other skills. No matter what you think of reading now, you will find that many if not all of the greatest minds in history were readers. Read my friend.

Remember the love,

Paul

25.

Earn Respect

Dear Paul,

Finally, we have arrived at immigrant advantage seven. As a bonus, I will send you one additional letter that is about something useful and cool, but is not an immigrant advantage. Who doesn't like to be useful and cool? Now let's get back to the topic of this letter. People use the term respect without understanding what it actually means. People throw around the word "respect" as if everybody deserves your respect. Not true! There are many peoples' opinions on the internet that claim you should respect everyone. This is a ridiculous notion. Now before you think of me as a callous unfeeling jackass, please hear me out and read on. We should treat everyone we meet with <u>civility</u> at a bare minimum. Civility is a form of courtesy and polite behavior. It would be great if we could be kind to one another in addition to being civil to each other. Kindness means that we as a society should be considerate and friendly to one another. This is sort of the next level above civility. Most of the people in my life are both civil and kind. The third tier in this hierarchy that I have been describing would be to respect all people we meet. The problem with respect is that unlike the first two ways of treating people that I mentioned, civility and kindness, respect can not be given, it must be earned. How can you respect anyone who you don't know? The answer: you can't. If you want respect from people, it is your job to earn it. If people want respect from you, they must earn it.

You actually learn about respect from the way people treat your parents. You realize that people are not always civil or kind to them, but they usually respect them for their hard work and dedication to getting their jobs done. When your father first immigrated to the United States, he became a plumber's apprentice, and he continued as a plumber's apprentice until he began his own business. People were always asking dad about how to fix plumbing problems. This is because he helped many friends and acquaintances fix plumbing issues, and he always did excellent work. These same people were not always civil to dad or even kind to him, but he helped them regardless. These people were ungrateful jackasses but my dad still helped them because that's the kind of person he is. I asked him one day why people who did not like him, kept asking him for help and he told me that these individuals respected his skills as a plumber. This is when you first learn that people could be cruel to you, and still respect you if you have earned their respect.

Please always be civil and kind to people; however, you don't have to respect everyone you meet immediately. Alternatively, if you want respect from someone, then earn it; it takes work like so many other things in life, but it is worth it.

Remember the love,

Paul

26.
How To
Get Strong

Dear Paul,

This final letter doesn't discuss immigrant advantages you have, but instead addresses how to train to become physically strong. This letter's purpose is to educate you so that you don't spend the early years of your strength training journey being the equivalent of the lead character in gym fail YouTube videos. You eventually do get strong, but the journey is a series of blunders that almost make you a candidate for the (you guessed it) Darwin Awards.

Because of your ability to make the simple complicated, a summary of how to train to become strong has been added to the middle of this letter. This summary acts like a short essay on Strength Training Secrets for Dummies. The founder of Starting Strength, Mark Rippetoe, eloquently states the reasons behind why everyone should be strong; "Being strong makes all other physical attributes better. Strength training makes you physically more useful, and it also makes you harder to kill". Please re-read this letter often; you'll save yourself a great deal of unnecessary stress.

So Paul, right now you are 16 years old about 5 feet 10 inches tall and weigh 140 lbs. and you have just discovered that weight training can make people bigger and stronger. This seems cool to you. You have watched the movie titled,"Pumping Iron," which made Arnold Schwarzenegger (The seven-time bodybuilding Mr. Olympia winner) famous. The guys in the movie are huge and jacked. You are so inspired by the movie that you go to the bookstore and find books on how to become a professional bodybuilder. You will buy the Arnold Schwarzenegger <u>Encyclopedia of Modern Bodybuilding</u>. You will start spending some of your money from your part-time job at the Italian Porkstore/Deli to buy a muscle magazine every month and follow what the magazine teaches you about gaining muscle and strength. You don't realize that most of the magazines highlight strength and bodybuilding routines that only people on anabolic steroids can use to get big and strong. You will be dedicated, because you love learning and improving yourself. You believe that in a short period you will be bench pressing three plates (315 pounds) and deadlifting 500 pounds. Well, it doesn't happen.

I am not trying to be discouraging here, but what I need you to understand is the fact that you (and many other people) don't always get it right on the first try. Also, on the off chance that you don't believe that it is indeed you who has been writing you all these letters with life lessons, remember the time when you were 12 years old, and you and your friends met the drunk guy at the baseball field and he played baseball with all of you. He called the special pitch he threw, "the Spliv." This guy was completely wasted, but definitely entertaining. Only six other humans on the planet were there, and only three other people actually will remember this event, especially the Spliv part.

In addition to what has been previously mentioned, here is what you will also do on this journey to become a physically stronger and more muscular you. You will buy a weight bench, 120 pounds of cement filled plastic weights, and you and your buddy will put it in his basement and make little progress using these weights. You don't understand the basics of progressive overload or lifting form, and you don't understand the difference between exercising and training. You will spend two hours per day five days per week focusing on too many exercises, most of which are isolation exercises such as bicep curls. By April of each of the first two years of your so-called-training, your progress will stall, so you and your buddy decide to take a few months off and since it's the end of the school year, and no one wants to train during the summer, you will begin training again in late September or early October.

This unproductive weight training process will continue for two years, and finally when you turn 18 years old, you will join Bally's Health Club, because you think that becoming part of a real gym will solve your training problems. By the way, Bally's is not my definition of a real gym. The original Gold's Gym in Venice Beach, California is a real hardcore gym, but I digress. You will spend a great deal of money on the gym membership, but you and your buddy think it's worth it. When you arrive at the health club, you walk by the aerobic step class, the pneumatic and Nautilus weight machines, as you head for the back room where the free weights are located. The free weight room is packed with massive humans, who are all strong and grunting. You have arrived at Nirvana and now imagine that you will get big and muscular like legendary bodybuilders Arnold Schwarzenegger, Franco Columbo (two time Mr. Olympia champion), and Lou Ferrigno (The Incredible Hulk from the T.V. Series) all of whom starred in Pumping Iron the movie. So before we continue with the letter, let me summarize the take-home messages for getting stronger. This summary is the most important part of this letter, so pay attention.

This summary statement <u>in part</u> captures most of the main ideas of gaining strength as written by the genius and strength coach, Mark Rippetoe. I have also added some other important information that I have learned through reading books, reading and doing research on strength training, and of course epically screwing up my strength training for a long time.

For a novice (someone who is far from their strength potential) to gain strength, you should train 3 days per week using correct form on compound, free weight movements (the barbell squat, deadlift, press, bench press, power cleans, pullups, and barbell rows). You must perform exercises that use the most muscle groups, using the most weight moving through the fullest range of motion, while progressing in weight on each of those movements, every training session for as long as you can. This process should last for 3-12 months before you become an intermediate lifter.

Eat 4-5 meals per day that contain 30-60 grams of protein, 20-30% fat, and enough carbohydrates so that you are in a caloric surplus and can gain weight. If you want to get strong, you must gain weight and some of that weight (about 33%-50%), will inevitably be fat weight. Ask yourself, do you want abs or do you want to be strong? If you want to be strong then this summary is all you need to know. If you want abs, you will need to use a different approach, one that usually does not involve gaining strength.

Our understanding of the importance of adequate sleep (8-10 hours/night) when strength training has recently increased, so I will briefly cover the topic without getting into the details about mechanisms and physiology. A person training for strength will place an extreme amount of stress on the body. This type of stress is not differentiated from any other type of stress. The body's job is to recover from all stress and be better or in the case of strength training, stronger after recovery than before the strength training session. This is because the human body is antifragile. Antifragile is a term coined by author Nassim Nicholas Taleb in his book *Antifragile: Things That Gain From Disorder*. Taleb writes, "Antifragility is beyond resilience or robustness. The resilient resists shocks and stays the same; the antifragile gets better." The correct dose of stress will actually make humans better, and in the case of strength training, stronger.

Rippetoe and Baker write about the stress, recovery, and adaptation cycle of getting stronger which is the process that allows humans to be antifragile. On pages 20-21 of their book *Practical Programming for Strength Training,* authors Rippetoe and Baker, make the case for the importance of sleep for recovery. The body is in the build and repair mode during sleep and a number of complicated physiologic changes occur, most importantly the increase in anabolic hormones (hormones that build) such as testosterone (anabolic to all tissue) and growth hormone (anabolic only to connective tissue) and a decrease in catabolic hormones (hormones that breakdown tissue for repair and for energy). Without adequate sleep not only, will a trainee fail to grow stronger, but will actually begin to feel run down and have more aches and pains in the major joints.

So in conclusion, get 8-10 hours of sleep every night. In contrast to the excellent advice of getting enough sleep when you train, remember that much of the information on the internet on how to get strong is either incorrect or at best suboptimal. Always find reliable sources such as the references cited in this letter for how to optimally build greater strength. Mark Rippetoe's Starting Strength group has optimized strength training better than any set of strength coaches in modern history. In addition, good coaches like those at StartingStrength.com are worth the fee, so get a good coach. Be well and if you are even feeling unsure about how to gain strength, read this letter again and read Rippetoe's books for detail.

Now let's get back to our story. You will actually make progress in gaining strength for a few months after joining Bally's Gym. You add some muscle and you will be able to do chest flyes with 70-pound dumbbells, impressive for a 150-pound kid. The problems will begin when your elbows and shoulders start to ache. You don't know it yet, but you are training too heavy too often, without a plan and without proper form, appropriate calories, and without enough sleep. You will end up herniating a vertebral disk in your cervical spine (neck) and will not be able to lift weights for two years. During this time in your life following all these injuries you will become a hot mess. Your college grades will drop into the toilet and you will simultaneously become extremely weak and frail.

Fast forward two years and you will eventually heal and move on towards building a career and a family and then continue to strength train somewhat non-productively for decades. Do yourself a favor and become educated about productive strength training and master the basics, and for the love of God, stop training like a dumbass. Read books written by people who actually understand training principles and methods. Those books would include <u>Super Strength</u> by Alan Calvert, <u>Physical Training Simplified</u> by Mark H. Berry, <u>Molding a Mighty Grip</u> by George F. Jowett, and <u>The Strongest Shall Survive: Strength Training for Football</u> by Bill Starr. These books were all written for normal, average genetics people, a.k.a. people who do not get paid millions of dollars to play sports or star in superhero movies. The principles and methods written about in these books work for all humans, not just the genetic freaks. Mark Rippetoe who is still very young during your time and who has been previously mentioned in the summary has not yet written the best strength training book ever, <u>Starting Strength Basic Barbell Training</u>. Look for this book and buy it as soon as you can and begin your productive journey of strength. In conclusion, don't be distracted by every new training plan and philosophy. Train hard and get strong my friend.

Remember the love,

Paul

27.

The Final Letter

Dear Reader,

All of the previous letters have been to our younger selves, but this one is specifically for you. In these letters, we have outlined strategies, skills, or perspectives we wish we'd known when we were younger. A lot of them have come from the "mistakes" we made in our youth; however, we now know that sage advice has no age limit to whom it may apply.

Each of us are certain that we would not be the people we are today without all of those experiences. None of the experiences, no matter how challenging, uncomfortable, or hard, was wasted. The great cosmic trick is to move through the experience and let go of the mental, emotional, and physical pain of knowing that you have failed at something. The beauty is that as you do learn to let go of the pain, you get to unwrap the gifts that were hidden there.

Without having lived through these mistakes, we would not have nearly the empathy, compassion, wisdom, and resilience that we have today. Everyone has these superpowers if you are willing to go on a journey to unlock them. To quote the late great Randy Pausch of The Last Lecture, "The best of the gold is at the bottom of the barrels of crap."

You don't need to embark on this journey alone. We are meant to grow stronger together. We, as a species, need each other. Find those people, both professionals and loved ones, who can guide and help you on this journey. Be patient with yourself and give yourself the time you need to grow. Tony Robbins, the famous self-help guru is fond of saying that most people over-estimate what they can do in a couple weeks, and underestimate what they can do in 5-10 years. If you stick with it, you may even find yourself being grateful for the experiences that shaped you. We know we are. We are grateful for the people that helped teach us and we are grateful for the situations/shit shows that led us to who we are supposed to be.

We are sure you have heard the expression that you are your own worst enemy, and we believe that some of the biggest hurdles in many people's lives are internal. However, the flipside of that saying is also true- you can be your own greatest hero. As you go through the process of shedding weakness and negative belief systems, implementing new strategies, and trusting yourself, you become your greatest source of strength. To quote a wonderful Disney song, "You are the one you've been waiting for."

Most of our lives are a journey of discovering who we are meant to be. After that, the journey is living it. The journey is the gift. May the journey be your joy.

We hope you enjoyed our group therapy session.

In service,

Paul

Justin

Nate

Get to Know the Authors

Paul

Paul Frank Martino was born in Brooklyn, New York in 1971, the eldest of two boys born to Italian immigrant parents, one of which came to the United States of America from the Molise Region of Italy, and the other came to the United States of America from the Naples (Campania) Region of Italy. Paul was raised as a practicing Roman Catholic in the town of Ronkonkoma, on Long Island, in the state of New York, and graduated from Connetquot High School, in Bohemia, New York in 1989. He graduated from Dowling College, in Oakdale, New York with a B.A. in Natural Sciences and Mathematics in 1993. He earned his Master's in Exercise Physiology from the Human Performance Laboratory at Ball State University, Muncie, Indiana in 1996, and later earned his Ph.D. in Physiology from the Medical College of Wisconsin in 2006. After earning, his Ph.D., Paul moved on to a two year American Heart Association, post-doctoral fellowship at Wright State University at the Boonshoft School of Medicine in the Department of Neuroscience, Cell Biology, and Physiology, studying the neuro-physiological effects of carbon dioxide regulation in the brain.

After his fellowship, he moved on to a short stay in the biomedical/pharmaceutical industry as a study director designing research studies for evaluating and understanding potential new drugs. During his stay in industry, he also simultaneously managed and mentored a small group of laboratory research technicians. He learned a great deal about managing and mentoring people in his short stint in industry. He also learned that the business side of research is very different from research in the academic world.

Since 2009, he has been a full-time tenure-track faculty member in the Biology Department at Carthage College, a small Lutheran affiliated liberal arts college in Kenosha, Wisconsin. He was awarded the prestigious "Teacher of the Year Award in 2017," for his outstanding teaching of Anatomy and Physiology to upper-classmen from across the Carthage campus. He currently leads the Carthage Biology Department as an Associate Professor and Chair. In addition, he also holds several other academic positions, which include Associate Adjunct Professor of Physiology at Medical College of Wisconsin, as well as a faculty member of the Stress and Motivated Institute (SMBI). He loves teaching and mentoring college students (Nate was one of my students.) to help them find their way in life, and has mentored 80 plus undergraduates in his active and collaborative research lab at Carthage. He has co-authored 21 peer-reviewed scientific articles on strength training, glucose metabolism, respiratory neurophysiology, sleep, antioxidants, and behavioral inhibition. His current research, which is in part a collaboration with Justin Miller and several other Carthage Syracuse and Northern Colorado University colleagues focuses on the physiology of college-age students who have the behavioral temperament called behavioral inhibition. This book signals a new stage of his professional life.

Justin

Justin Robert Miller was born in Maywood, Illinois in 1985. His father is a successful veterinarian near Chicago, and his mother was a stay-at-home parent to Justin and his brother, which should automatically qualify her for sainthood. He was raised in the northwest suburbs of Chicago where he spent most of his early years being a fat kid, but got in shape by wrestling throughout grade school and high school. He graduated from William Fremd High School in 2003, and became a novice-level competitive bodybuilder taking 1st place in the NPC Mid-Illinois Bodybuilding Competition mixed pair division with his mother in 2004.

He graduated from Northern Illinois University in Dekalb, Illinois with a B.S. in Biological Sciences in 2007, and earned his Doctorate in Physiology from the Medical College of Wisconsin in Milwaukee, Wisconsin in 2013. After earning his Ph.D. Justin completed two years of post-doctoral studies at the Milwaukee Veterans Affairs Hospital in the Department of Anesthesia Research studying opiate sensitive areas of the brainstem. He has co-authored 12 peer-reviewed scientific articles studying respiratory neurophysiology, brain plasticity, opiate effects on breathing, and behavioral inhibition.

Since 2015, he has been a full time faculty member in the Biology Department at Carthage College with Paul Martino. He currently teaches anatomy and physi-ology classes for health professionals at Carthage, and a one-month beer brewing class during J-terms. He is a research collaborator with Paul also studying the effects of behavioral inhibition among college age students.

Justin and his wife Therese have two daughters, Evelyn and Fiona ages 7 and 2 who are always providing inspiration for his writing. He takes great pride in being a dad and enjoys spending time outdoors with his family. He also enjoys fishing, automotive restoration, and brewing beer although most of his free time is spent fighting never-ending battles against diapers, dishes, cat hair, and chin fat. He is excited to share some of his stories and hopes he can help others develop tools for success, while also enjoying life.

Nate

Dr. Nathan Paul Gerowitz, a family chiropractor, heeds a deep calling to help people unconditionally love themselves and participate in life. He was born in the suburbs of Chicago in 1990. His father, Rob, is one of the world's leading experts in Orthokeratology, regularly lecturing around the globe. His mother, Korreen, is the CFO of three companies all while supporting Rob, Nathan, and Miranda in anything they desired to achieve.

After graduating from William Fremd High school in 2009, he attended Carthage College in Kenosha, WI. It was here that he met Paul and Justin. In 2011, he went to Nicaragua for the first time, participating in Carthage's J-term class. Upon returning, his class began building a non-profit organization to create sustainable, clean water for the island of Ometepe. This organization, Carthage World Relief, is still operating today. After graduating with honors in 2013, Nathan moved to Marietta, GA to attend Life University.

Whilst completing his Doctor of Chiropractic degree, he regularly attended advanced seminars in the art, science, and practice of chiropractic. In 2015, he began serving as a facilitator for MLS Adjusting Seminars. He continues that service today, teaching students and doctors to serve with integrity, ease, and authenticity. During his time in Georgia, Nathan also became a practitioner of Divine Intervention and Spontaneous Remission, and Quickening: Accelerated Conscious Evolution, a shamanic healing art and shadow processing modality respectively.

After briefly serving in southern California, Nathan returned to his hometown and founded Innate Life Chiropractic. His focus is on helping families to heal, grow, and thrive through vitalistic chiropractic care. He lives in the suburbs of Chicago with his partner Maddie and their dog Milly.

Acknowledgments

Paul

I would like to thank the many people who have made my journey in life worth the ride. First, I would like to thank my parents Nick and Teresa who are my biggest heroes. To my brother Steve, I say "Pooh Dog." I love you and am proud of the man and father you have become. Thanks for always having my back. To my wife of 22 years, Karen, thank you for always supporting my career. To our beautiful daughters Kate and Claire, you are the greatest joys and accomplishments of my life; I hope that both of you keep bringing joy to all whose lives you touch.

Further, I would like to thank all my mentors and colleagues including Bruce W. Craig Ph.D., Bert V. Forster Ph.D., Robert W. Putnam, Ph.D., Matthew R. Hodges, Ph.D., Patrick "Mupfaffle" K. Pfaffle, Ph.D., Elaine Radwanski, Ph.D., Daniel P. Miller, Ph.D., and Matthew "Crush" Zorn, Ph.D. You have all made me a better professional.

To Elaine Radwanski, Ph.D., and Denise Cook-Snyder, Ph.D., Thank you for the valuable feedback while preparing this book. I would like to thank my two brothers with whom I have co-authored this book. I love you both and cherish our brotherhood, friendship, and thank you for taking this journey with me and writing our first book, together. Finally, I would like to thank all the wonderful students who I have been blessed to teach (the greatest of whom has been Nate Gerowitz, one of my co-authors) and to get to know over the last 12 years; getting to know all of you and watching you grow as people has been my honor. God bless all of you.

Justin

I would like to thank my parents Bob and Sue who have both taught me what a mature work ethic should look like. You have both taught me how to be a hard-working and compassionate person. I would also like to thank Brad, Dave and Karen who continuously mentor me as one of their own. In addition, I would like to thank my beautiful wife Therese, who has very graciously put up with me for 15 years, and always makes sure that my life has a healthy dose of "adventure." To my daughters Evelyn and Fiona- thank you for being a constant source of joy and inspiration, and ensuring that each passing day is worth the struggle. I would also like to thank my brother Tom- I am proud of the man you have become. Finally, I would like to thank my friend Luke Woods for the valuable insight while preparing and editing this book.

Nate

I am who I am today because of the beautiful, amazing people in my life, such as my loving, fun, supportive family. Rob, my dad is my best friend. Korreen, my mom is the rock for all of us. Miranda, my sister is the greatest demonstration of living passionately that I have known.

Profound gratitude to my extended family who love and support me in body; Grammy & Marty, Loren & David, Char & Gigi. In addition, for my family that is in Spirit, Don, Nana, Martin, Papa Nathan, Aunt Paula, and Marion.

Maddie, my girlfriend and partner, who supports my highest aspirations. Thank you for the life we are co-creating.

One of the greatest blessings of my life is the family I've found along the way. Those with whom I grew up. The family I found at a small school called Carthage, who walked with me during immense joy and grief, refreshing my soul as we went. Moreover, my brothers and sisters from Life who journeyed with me into a world of infinite potential. I love you all.

Deep appreciation to my teachers and mentors: Patton, Paul, Crush, MuPfaffle, Suzan, Wade, Arno, Katina, Lou, Eric, John, Sue, Pam, and Chad.

In addition, I'd like to thank all who allow me to help them live healthy, vibrant, connected lives. It's an honor and a privilege.

Suggested Reading

These reading suggestions are for those who want to explore the topics of these letters more deeply.

JUSTIN'S LETTERS

1. Struggling

No additional readings suggested as these are all my own thoughts.

2. Failure

Adams, Scott, 2013, How to Fail at Almost Everything and Still Win Big: Kind of the Story of My Life, Portfolio, ISBN: 9780241003701.

Day, Elizabeth, 2020, How to Fail: Everything I've Learned from Things Going Wrong, Fourth Estate, ISBN-10: 0008327351.

Goggins, David, 2018, Can't Hurt Me: Master Your Mind and Defy the Odds, Lioncrest Publishing, ISBN-10: 1544512287.

Harford, Tim, 2011, Adapt: Why Success Always Starts with Failure, Farrar, Straus, and Giroux, ISBN-10: 0374100969.

Willink Jocko and Babin Leif, 2017, Extreme Ownership: How U.S. Navy SEALS Lead and Win, St. Martin's Press, ISBN: 9781250183866.

3. Self-Discipline

Furtick, Steven, 2012, Greater, Multnomah Books, ISBN: 9781601426550

4. Meekness: Quiet Strength

No additional readings suggested as these are all my own thoughts.

5. Speaking Without Getting Punched in the Face Immediately

Voss, Chris, 2017, Never Split the Difference, ISBN-13: 978-1847941497

6. Emailing Without Getting Punched in the Face Later

No additional readings suggested as these are all my own thoughts.

7. Success At Long Last

Willink Jocko and Babin Leif, 2017, Extreme Ownership: How U.S. Navy SEALS Lead and Win, St. Martin's Press, ISBN: 9781250183866.

Goggins, David, 2018, Can't Hurt Me: Master Your Mind and Defy the Odds, Lioncrest Publishing, ISBN-10: 1544512287.

Willink Jocko, 2017, Discipline Equals Freedom: Field Manual, St. Martin's Press, ISBN-10: 9781250156945.

Peterson B. Jordan, 2018, 12 Rules for Life: An Antidote to Chaos, Random House Canada, ISBN-10: 0345816021.

Weinman, Sam, 2016, Win at Losing: How Our Biggest Setbacks Can Lead to Our Greatest Gains, TarcherPerigree, ISBN-10: 0143109588

8. Having Kids

Dancy, Rahima Baldwin, 2012, You Are Your Child's First Teacher, ISBN-13: 978-1607743026

Berkus, Rusty, 1984, Appearances: Clearings Through the Masks of Our Existence, ISBN-13: 978-0960988815

NATE'S LETTERS

9. Reason Versus Purpose

Port, Dr. Wade - Atlanta, GA - Chiropractor and Teacher

Rossi, Dr. Suzan - Atlanta, GA - Chiropractor and Teacher

Sinek, Simon, 2011, Start With Why, ISBN-13: 978-1591846444

Sinek, Simon, 2017, Find Your Why, ISBN-13: 978-0143111726

Movie mentioned: The Shawshank Redemption (1994)

10. Fear Of Being Wrong

Holiday, Ryan, 2014, The Obstacle is the Way: The Timeless Art of Turning Trials into Triumphs, Portfolio, ISBN: 9781781251492.

Vaynerchuk Gary, 2016, #Ask Gary Vee: One Entrepreneur's Take on Leadership, Social Media, and Self-Awareness, Harper Business, ISBN-10: 9780062273123.

11. Gratitude

Lally, P., Jaarsveld, C. H., Potts, H. W., & Wardle, J. (2009). How are habits formed: Modelling habit formation in the real world. European Journal of Social Psychology, 40(6), 998-1009. doi:10.1002/ejsp.674

Kevorkian, Dr. Peter - Westwood, MA - Chiropractor and Teacher
https://www.youtube.com/watch?v=HEOfsTCzSsE

12. Don't Go It Alone

Sinek, Simon, 2017, Leaders Eat Last, ISBN-13: 978-1591848011

Brown, Brené, 2019, Dare to Lead, ISBN-13: 978-0593171127

Jackson, Phil, 2014, Eleven Rings, ISBN-13: 978-0143125341

13. Water, Water, Water

Batmanghelidj, Fereydoon, 2003, Water: For Health, for Healing, for Life: You're Not Sick, You're Thirsty! ISBN-13: 978-0446690744

14. Rest

No additional readings suggested as these are all my own thoughts.

15. Shadow Dancing In A Global Crisis

Jung, Carl - Swiss Psychiatrist

Rossi, Dr. Suzan - Atlanta, GA - Master Healer & Chiropractor - drsuzan.com

Adams, Dennis - Mt. Shasta, CA - Master Healer & Teacher - dennisadamsmasterhealer.com

Lipton PhD, Bruce H., 2016, The Biology of Belief, ISBN-13: 978-1401952471

Pert, Candace B., 1999, Molecules of Emotion, ISBN-13: 978-0684846347

Karpinski, Gloria, 1990, Where Two Worlds Touch, ISBN-13: 978-0345353313

Brown, Sue, BGI - Position Statement & Subluxation Defined, https://youtu.be/qiOwuoEIaKs

Ruiz, Don Miguel, 2018, The Four Agreements, ISBN-13: 978-1878424310

16. Magic In Your Body

Corleto, Louis, 2011, Healing vs Curing, ISBN-13: 978-1461079156

Corleto, Louis, Conscious Breathing, Online class,
https://www.loucorleto.com/store/hPcBRj22

Fleet, Thurman, 2000, Rays of the Dawn, ISBN: 978-0-9671845-0-0

Haavik, Heidi, 2019, The Reality Check, ISBN-13: 978-0473470432

Barham-Floreani, Jennifer, 2008, Well-Adjusted
Babies, ISBN-13: 978-0975786017

LaMarche, Gilles A., 2016, The Art of Being
Healthy, ISBN-13: 978-0989843027

van der Kolk M.D., Bessel, 2015, The Body Keeps the Score: Brain, Mind,
and Body in the Healing of Trauma, ISBN-13 : 978-0143127741

Epstein, Donald, 2000, Healing Myths, Healing
Magic, ISBN-13: 978-1878424396

Epstein, Donald, 1994, The 12 Stages of Healing, ISBN-13: 978-1878424082

Hof, Wim, 2020, The Wim Hof Method, ISBN-13: 978-1683644095

Upledger, John E., 1997, Your Inner Physician
and You, ISBN-13: 978-1556432460

Porges, Stephan W., 2011, The Polyvagal Theory, ISBN-13: 978-0393707007

Chopra, Deepak, 2019, Metahuman, ISBN-13: 978-1846046087

Rondberg, Terry A, 1998, Chiropractic First, ISBN: 964716828

17. Life Is Cumulative

No additional readings suggested as these are all my own thoughts.

PAUL'S LETTERS

18. Think Like the Successful Child of Immigrants

Vaynerchuk Gary, 2016, #Ask Gary Vee: One Entrepreneur's Take on Leadership, Social Media, and Self-Awareness, Harper Business, ISBN-10: 9780062273123.

19. Make More Good Decisions Than Bad Decisions for a Successful Life

Deida, David, 2017 (Reprint), The Way of the Superior Man: A Spiritual Guide to Mastering the Challenges of Women, Work, and Sexual Desire, Sounds True, ISBN: 9781591792574

McRaven, William H., Admiral (Ret.), 2017, Make Your Bed: Little Things That Can Change Your Life and Maybe the World (2nd Edtion), Grand Central Publishing, ISBN-10: 1455570249.

Frankl, Viktor E., 1959 (Revised Edition), Man's Search for Meaning, Beacon Press, ISBN-10: 0807060100.

https://darwinawards.com/

20. Don't Be Thin Skinned

Brokaw, Tom, 2004, The Greatest Generation, Random House, ISBN-10: 140

Holiday, Ryan, 2014, The Obstacle is the Way: The Timeless Art of Turning Trials into Triumphs, Portfolio, ISBN: 9781781251492

Peterson B. Jordan, 2018, 12 Rules for Life: An Antidote to Chaos, Random House Canada, ISBN-10: 0345816021.

Seneca, James S. Romm (translator), 2019, How to Keep Your Cool: An Ancient Guide to Anger Management (Ancient Wisdom for Modern Readers), Princeton University Press, ISBN: 9780691181950.

Schuller, Robert H., 1984, Tough Times Never Last, but Tough People Do! Bantam, Reissue Edition, ISBN-10 0553273329.

Taleb, Nassim Nicholas, 2012, Antifragile: Things that Gain from Disorder, Random House Publishing Group, ISBN: 0812979680.

Willink Jocko and Babin Leif, 2017, Extreme Ownership: How U.S. Navy SEALS Lead and Win, St. Martin's Press, ISBN: 9781250183866.

Vaynerchuk Gary, 2016, #Ask Gary Vee: One Entrepreneur's Take on Leadership, Social Media, and Self-Awareness, Harper Business, ISBN-10: 9780062273123.

21. Live Within Your Means

No additional readings suggested as these are all my own thoughts.

22. Chase Contentment, Not Happiness

Aurelius, Marcus, (translated by George Long with an introduction by Andrew Fiala) (1909 originally published, 2003, Meditations, Barnes & Noble, New York, ISBN: 978076075229-6.

Frankl, Viktor E., 1959 (Revised Edition), Man's Search for Meaning, Beacon Press, ISBN-10: 0807060100.

23. Work Hard

Goggins, David, 2018, Can't Hurt Me: Master Your Mind and Defy the Odds, Lioncrest Publishing, ISBN-10: 1544512287.

Lukianoff, Greg, and Haidt, Jonathan, 2018, The Coddling of the American Mind: How Good Intentions and Bad Ideas are Setting up a Generation for Failure, Penguin Books, ISBN: 9780735224896.

Musk, Elon, 2017, Elon Musk: Tesla, SpaceX and the Quest for a Fantastic ISBN: 006230125X

Vaynerchuk, Gary, 2016, #Ask Gary Vee: One Entrepreneur's Take on Leadership, Social Media, and Self-Awareness, Harper Business, ISBN-10: 9780062273123.

Willink Jocko and Babin Leif, 2017, Extreme Ownership: How U.S. Navy SEALS Lead and Win, St. Martin's Press, ISBN: 9781250183866.

Willink Jocko, 2017, Discipline Equals Freedom: Field Manual, St. Martin's Press, ISBN-10: 9781250156945.

24. Read Often

Billington, J., Dowrick, C. Hamer, 2017, An investigation into the Therapeutic Benefits of reading in Relation to Depression and Well-being, The Reader.

Cullinan, B. E., 2000, Independent Reading and School Achievement, School Library Media Research, Research Journal of American Association of School Librarians, 3, ISSN: 1523-4320.

Ferriss, T., 2017, How to speed read: Tim Ferriss

https://www.youtube.com/watch?v=ZwEquW_Yij0

Garan, E.M., DeVoogd, G., 2008, The Benefits of Sustained Silent Reading: Scientific Research and Common Sense Coverage, Reading Teacher, 62(4): 336-344.

Tozcu, J., Coady, J., 2004, Successful Learning of Frequent Vocabulary Through CALL Also Benefits Reading Comprehension and Speed, Computer Assisted Language Learning, 17(5): 473-495.

Vadsay, P.F., Sanders, E.A- Remedial and Special Education, 2008,Benefits of repeated reading intervention for low-achieving fourth-and fifth-grade students, Remedial and Special Education, 29(4): 235-249.

Wilson, R.L, Boyle, P.A, Yu, L., Barnes, L.L., Schneider, J.A, Bennett, D.A. 2013, Life-span Cognitive Activity, Neuropathologic Burden, and Cognitive Aging, Neurology, 81(4): 314–321.

Whitten, C., Labby, S., Sullivan, S. 2016, The Impact of reading on Academic Success, The Journal of Multidisciplinary Graduate Research, 2(4): 48-64.

25. Earn Respect

Brokaw, Tom, 2004, The Greatest Generation, Random House, ISBN-10: 140

Willink Jocko and Babin Leif, 2017, Extreme Ownership: How U.S. Navy SEALS Lead and Win, St. Martin's Press, ISBN: 9781250183866.

26. How To Get Strong

Berry, Mark H., 1920, Physical Training Simplified by Milo Publishing, Philadelphia.

Calvert Alan, (1924 original publication) 2013, Super Strength, CreateSpace Independent Publishing Platform, ISBN: 148196092X.

Helms Eric, Ph.D., Morgan, B.S., Valdez Andrea, M.S., 2019, The Muscle and Strength Pyramid: Training, Independently Published, ISBN-10: 109091282X.

Jowett, George F., (1930 original publication) 2011, Molding a Mighty Grip by StrongmanBooks.com.

Rippetoe Mark, 2013, Starting Strength Basic Barbell Training 3rd Edition, The Aasgaard Company, Wichita Falls, Texas.

Rippetoe Mark and Baker Andy, 2013, Practical Programming for Strength Training 3rd Edition, The Aasgaard Company, Wichita Falls, Texas.

Taleb Nassim Nicholas, 2012, Antifragile: Things That Gain From Disorder, Random House, New York

PAUL, JUSTIN, AND NATE

27. The Final Letter

Pausch, Randy - Professor Carnegie Mellon - The Last Lecture
https://www.youtube.com/watch?v=ji5_MqicxSo

Bregman, Rutger, 2020, Humankind, ISBN-13: 978-0316418539

Brown, Brené 2012, The Power of Vulnerability, ASIN: B00D1Z9RFU (Audiobook)

Coelho, Paulo, 2014, The Alchemist, ISBN-13: 978-0062315007